TRUMP
THE ART OF SURVIVAL

DONALD J. TRUMP
with CHARLES LEERHSEN

WARNER BOOKS

A Time Warner Company

All photographs courtesy the Trump Organization
unless otherwise indicated.

WARNER BOOKS EDITION

Copyright © 1990 by Donald J. Trump
All rights reserved.

This Warner Books Edition is published by arrangement with
Random House, Inc., 201 East 50th Street, New York, N.Y. 10022

Cover photo by Harry Benson
Cover design by Robert Aulicino

Warner Books, Inc.
666 Fifth Avenue
New York, N.Y. 10103

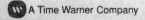 A Time Warner Company

Printed in the United States of America

First Warner Books Printing: August, 1991

10 9 8 7 6 5 4 3 2 1

INSIDE
THE ART
OF SURVIVAL

On survival: "One reason I'm still around, while others aren't, is that I see nothing as cast in stone, whether it's the way a deal is structured or the design of a building. I'm always open to suggestion, even fairly radical ones."

On pragmatism: "I expect to succeed, always and in all things, or I wouldn't attempt them in the first place. But I never expect to be perfect. I always know in the back of my mind that for one reason or another I may have to make major changes, or even totally abandon the project in hand, and move on to one of the five or six other projects I'm always sure to have going."

On insecurity: "When you're insecure you're usually not feeling bold and brash enough to try something new. Sometimes pride and sheer stubbornness are to blame. But if you look around and check the record, you'll see that survivors don't dig in their heels; they're light on their feet."

On the future: "Anyone who thinks my story is anywhere near over is sadly mistaken."

Also by Donald J. Trump

TRUMP: THE ART OF THE DEAL

Published by
WARNER BOOKS

For Steve, Mark, and Jon

ACKNOWLEDGMENTS

When my good friend Si Newhouse, the owner of Random House, suggested that I write my first book, I was wary. The last thing I needed was to do a book about myself that went nowhere. Si was confident because he had noticed that when my picture appeared on the covers of magazines he owned, they became top sellers. Si is a very persistent man, and I was flattered by his interest. "Okay," I finally said, "let's do it."

Peter Osnos, associate publisher of Random House and an experienced and talented editor, went to work on the book with me, and we were joined by the writer Tony Schwartz. Si was right; the book turned out to be one of the biggest publishing successes in recent years. After it was published in 1987, *The Art of the Deal* spent thirty-two weeks on *The New York Times* best-seller list, many of them as number one. Then it was on the paperback best-seller list for nineteen weeks, seven of them in the number-one position. What many thought was just a New York book wound up being translated into more than a dozen languages and became an international best-seller. On the whole, the public here and abroad has shown great warmth toward me since the book came out. Looking back on it, I see that writing *The Art of the Deal* was one of the most satisfying and fulfilling experiences of my life.

Peter and I had to find another writer this time because Tony was involved with other projects. We chose Charles Leerhsen, a senior writer at *Newsweek*, who from the start shared our view that this second book should not simply continue the story of my major deals but should be a more personal work.

I've scored some of the biggest victories of my career since my first book, but I've also faced some obstacles that taught me not to take the winning for granted. That's why I decided to call this book *Surviving at the Top*.

I hope you enjoy it and can profit from it. I know that this book offers not only better business advice but also, to my way of thinking, more lessons from life and the problems of fame and fortune.

D.J.T.

Charles Leerhsen wishes to thank a number of people whose help was invaluable during the writing of this book, especially Joni Evans, Robert Trump, Harvey Freeman, Blanche Sprague, John Bernstein, Susan Heilbron, Richard Wilhelm, Jeff Walker, Barbara Res, Rhona Graff, Carol Schneider, Virginia Avery, Bob

Aulicino, Carole Lowenstein, Linda Kaye, Eve Adams, Bernie Klein, Mitchell Ivers, Jane Henning, Jenny Jackson, Matthew Calamari, Brian Baudreau, John Barry, Sal Alfano, Janet Kellock of Professional Transcription Services, and the legendary literary agent Kris Dahl—as well as Erica, Deborah, and Nora Leerhsen. A special debt of gratitude is due Norma Foerderer, who provided hard facts and sage wisdom—and cleared the way for the many lengthy creative sessions with Donald Trump that made this book possible.

The credit belongs to the man who is actually in the arena; whose face is marred by dust and sweat; who strives valiantly; who errs and may fail again and again, because there is no effort without error or shortcoming; but who does actually strive to do the deeds, who does know the great enthusiasm, the great devotion.

—THEODORE ROOSEVELT

You don't have no fun at all, you know, if you get *too* famous.

—LOUIS ARMSTRONG

CONTENTS

TRUMP
THE ART OF SURVIVAL

A NEW INTRODUCTION
FOR THE
PAPERBACK EDITION

"Tough times don't last," Robert Schuller once said, "but tough people do."

A lot has happened since this book came out in hardcover. Some of it has been extremely challenging. The drastic change in the business climate as the 1980s drew to a close has led me to rethink some of my strategy and style. It's made me work harder, and it's taught me who my friends are—and aren't.

A lot has been written about me since the economy took a turn for the worse. One thing that amazes me about what is written is that I often wind up taking the heat for what is happening to literally thousands of other businesspeople. I don't care what the government economists call it: we've been experiencing not just a recession, but outright depression in this country, especially in the Northeast. If you don't believe me, ask the many real estate developers who've been totally devastated. And if you still think *depression* is too strong a term for what's been going on in the economy, then consider Pan Am, which has fallen so far that it had to file for bankruptcy—or Eastern, a once-proud airline that has vanished from the scene forever.

The rapid downward spiral that started at the end

of the '80s has been a worldwide phenomenon. I agree with those economists who say that we've lately been experiencing the worst recession since World War II. But I learned back in my days at the Wharton School that economics is known as the dismal science. As vital as it is to so many aspects of life, as central as it is to understanding world history, it doesn't sell newspapers or magazines or bring in big TV ratings on sweeps week. So the media ignores the real issues and concentrates instead on a high-profile personality such as myself.

Fine. The press can be fair, and in covering me it often is. But oversimplification and distortion are often part of the way the media game is played. If your business interests put you in the limelight, the way mine do, you've got to accept that fact of life and move on. But one thing my critics have never understood about me is that tough times don't depress me. They energize me.

Looking back, I see that one of the least happy periods of my life was when the '80s mentality was at its peak, and borrowing money was incredibly easy and many of my business interests seemed to almost manage themselves. The press then, with only a few exceptions, was adoring; no matter what the situation, they would take my side of the story without question, often to the point where it sometimes made even me feel a little uneasy. The media's methods often caused me to wonder if what I was getting from them, as a reader and a viewer, was objective truth or something else entirely—something that had more to do with their whims, fads, and current darlings.

In any case, everything was going my way. But I couldn't enjoy myself. I was eager for new challenges. And, as things turned out, I got them.

Right now for example, as I prepare this book for publication, I'm working out a variety of situations in creative, constructive ways. Consider what's happened with the extremely valuable property I own along the West Side rail yards. I have worked out a plan with New York City officials and local civic and community organizations that will be not just satisfactory but also genuinely exciting and beneficial for all concerned. Once, all you heard about this project was that it was opposed by this group or that. But in a recent story in the *New York Times*, a real estate expert who is advising the West Side residents was quoted as saying, "I think everybody understands what a compelling idea the project is. It is not only clearly in the public's interest, but probably also in the developer's. The idea of taking conflict away from a process that is usually contentious in New York is very appealing." Thanks to the cooperation of many people, including Mayor David Dinkins and strong endorsements from community groups, civic leaders and architectural critics, I'm sure this real estate will in the near future become a residential and commercial area of which New York can be truly proud.

Another recent project I'm very excited about is the redevelopment of Mar-a-Lago, my home in Palm Beach. The seventeen-acre Mar-a-Lago estate is a truly magnificent piece of real estate—and it was an equally magnificent bargain when I bought it. As time went on, and my life changed, however, it became clear to me that this historic and unique piece of property could be put to better use. The plan I came up with calls for a subdivision of the gorgeous Mar-a-Lago land into separate homesites, each of which will have a house inspired by the mostly Mediterranean design of the main mansion. It's an idea that's right for the area and right for the times.

As for Atlantic City, my faith in that town remains unshaken. I point out in a later chapter of this book that Atlantic City, despite being the number-one tourist destination in America, has many problems, some of which date back to the pregambling era. Since this book was published in hardcover, though, the Casino Control Commission and various other local officials have announced plans to expand and modernize the town's main airport so that it can handle traffic from the major airlines. This is an important step in the process of upgrading Atlantic City as a major resort and tourist destination.

There is a lesson in all this, by the way, about the often misunderstood art of survival. When times are relatively hard, you, as a businessperson, have got to be flexible. One reason I'm still around while others aren't is that I see nothing as cast in stone, whether it's the way a deal is structured or the design of a building. I'm always open to suggestion, even fairly radical ones, if it makes sense financially and aesthetically.

Dealing with changing circumstances does allow for satisfactions that don't come otherwise. If you're successful at what you're doing, the experience can on some level even be considered fun. After all, what are golf and tennis except activities in which you have to adapt to ever-changing circumstances? If there were no challenge, there would be no game.

The truth is, though, I've had to learn to think that way. There is a part of everyone's nature, including mine, that is resistant to change. It doesn't matter how the situation seems to be crying out for a new approach: people instinctively dig in their heels and stick to their original plan, even if it's to their own detriment. This is true of an inflexible businessperson who can't abandon a bad plan or idea. That captain of industry usually winds up going down with his or her ship.

Sometimes pride and sheer stubbornness are to blame. Often, though, I suspect this happens because adversity often leads to feelings of insecurity, and when you're insecure you're usually not feeling bold and brash enough to try something new. But whatever the reason for that feeling, I've taught myself to react less instinctively. If you look around and check the record you'll see that survivors don't dig in their heels; they're light on their feet.

One good way to get and stay in this frame of mind, I think, is to keep a constant check on your expectations. "Every war is going to astonish you," Dwight D. Eisenhower once said.

I expect to succeed, always and in all things, or I wouldn't attempt them in the first place. But I never expect to be perfect. I go into a project knowing that unforeseen circumstances are bound to crop up, and some things are bound to go wrong. No matter how confident I seem, I always know in the back of my mind that for one reason or another I may have to make major changes, or even totally abandon the project in hand, and move on to one of the five or six other projects I'm always sure to have going.

This is the mind-set of the professional prize-fighter—an excellent model for anyone interested in the art of survival. If you look at any green schoolboy in the annual Golden Gloves tournament, for example, and compare him to a seasoned veteran of the ring, you'll see what I mean. The amateur may be a brash kid from the meanest streets of Brooklyn or the South Bronx, the kind of guy who intimidates people just by walking down the street. But probably the first time he gets hit by an opponent in the ring, he goes crazy, flailing away at his rival in a way that wastes energy or leaves him open for further attack. Either that or he goes into a shell, pulling up his arms and ducking his head down, a position from which he invites further punishment. I've seen it happen a thousand times. Like the instinct to stay with the status quo, this too is human nature.

The truly professional fighter, in contrast, has disciplined himself away from that reaction. He expects some adversity, no matter how macho his attitude before the bell sounds. He knows, going in, that the other guy is going to be throwing shots his way, and that there's no reason to take it personally or to panic. And when those fists finally do come flying, he, being a skilled survivor, knows what to do. He bobs, he weaves, he rolls with the punches.

So do I. Though, also like the professional fighter, I know that while I'm doing this I also must be throwing shots, so to speak, of my own.

One lesson I've had reinforced in the recent past is that there is absolutely no shame in making adjustments. Having high standards and confidence is one thing. But no one is perfect, and perfectionism, as I see it, is a character flaw that can ultimately lead to disaster.

I believe William Faulkner said it brilliantly when he wrote, "All of us failed to match our dream of perfection. So I rate us on the basis of our splendid failure to do the impossible. In my opinion, if I could write my work again, I am convinced that I would do it better, which is the healthiest condition for an artist. That's why he keeps on working, trying again. . . ."

Of course, making a change in the interest of getting a little closer to perfection is not always painless. Sometimes, even if you're rolling with it, the punch hurts, and there's nothing you can do but tough it out.

And now one final word of caution. As important as the willingness to change is, sometimes you've got to stand and fight.

Anyone who thinks my story is anywhere near over is sadly mistaken. Like this book, it's just getting started.

—DJT, March 1991

PART
I

PART
I

ONE

NOW FOR THE HARD PART

A helicopter crashes, and several good friends are suddenly dead.

A marriage goes stale after twelve years.

A heavyweight champ in whose career you were involved, and who everyone thought was invincible, hits the canvas in a heap, not far from where you are sitting.

The business climate changes, and the so-called experts start questioning whether you've lost your touch. You know damn well you haven't. But you also know, better than most people, that perception is reality. And so you've got a job on your hands.

* * *

It doesn't matter whether you have three billion or three hundred dollars in the bank: Life is a series of challenges. Some of the challenges you face turn out well. Some don't. What separates the winners from the losers, I've learned—in business and any other aspect of life—is how a person reacts to each twist of fate. You have to be confident as you face the world each day, but you can't be too cocky. Anyone who thinks he's going to win them all is going to wind up a big loser.

This is Phase Two of my life, in which the going gets a lot tougher and the victories, because they are harder won, seem all the sweeter.

The last three years have been for me a time of extraordinary challenges—successes and setbacks. I bought and restored to greatness the Plaza Hotel, a New York landmark. I acquired the run-down Eastern Shuttle and made it, as the Trump Shuttle, the best airline of its kind. I erected the magnificent Taj Mahal, one of the largest casino-hotels in the world—and a project that many experts predicted could never be completed.

In one sense, I continued doing what I have always been good at: acquiring new properties and following my instincts into new and varied fields; making deals and waging business wars.

But not all the news was positive.

In both my private and my business life I encountered some rough times. As a result, I'm not the same person that I was just a few years ago. The changes I've undergone—and the amazing things that I've seen happen along the way—are what this book is about.

I think it's vitally important, during times of pressure, to face up to reality, however unpleasant that may be. We live in an age when huge corporations and important investors are in the midst of major restructuring. Business runs in cycles, and even the eighties had to come to an end.

The 1980s were, of course, the so-called go-go years of leveraged buyouts and megamergers—a time when almost any entrepreneur with a good track record could raise huge sums of money from banks, or from the sale of junk bonds, with unprecedented ease. It was also a time when "acquiring" became synonymous with "winning."

When I attended the Wharton School I learned that buying low and selling high was basically what business was all about. During the last decade, though, a different mentality often prevailed, and anyone who backed down after showing an interest in any sort of asset was considered a loser. It used to bug the hell out of me when I'd drop out of the bidding for something and then get a call from a reporter asking, "So, Mr. Trump, how does it feel to get beat?"

I knew the real loser was the guy who overpaid.

And yet to a certain extent I got caught up in the buying frenzy myself—although even my critics must admit I wound up with some truly world-class assets. Looking back, I see that there were two reasons for what happened, apart from the fact that the required money was always available. The first reason is that I'm sometimes too competitive for my own good. If someone is going around labeling people winners and losers, I want to play the game and, of course, come out on the right side.

The other reason is that I get bored too easily. My attention span is short, and probably my least favorite thing to do is to maintain the status quo. Instead of being content when everything is going fine, I start getting impatient and irritable.

So I look for more and more deals to do. On a day in which I've got several good ones in the works and the phone calls and faxes are going back and forth and the tension is palpable—well, at those times I feel the way other people do when they're on vacation.

This has led to some misunderstanding. Many people have called me greedy because of the way I amassed real estate, companies, helicopters, planes, and yachts during the last several years. But what those critics don't know is that the same assets that excite me in the chase often, once they are acquired, leave me bored. I probably visited Mar-a-Lago, my 118-room house in Palm Beach, no more than two dozen times in the years I've owned it. As for my yacht, the

Trump Princess, it is a dazzling trophy and a terrific business tool, but it never really became part of my personal life.

For me, you see, the important thing is the getting . . . not the having.

That's why it hasn't bothered me much that, largely because the Atlantic City casino market went somewhat soft and my properties there generated less cash than I had counted on, I had to restructure my holdings and generally streamline my operations and my lifestyle. Matters came to a head in the spring. Over several weeks of very hard bargaining, my bankers and I worked out a terrific deal that allows me the time, the money, and the leeway to come out stronger than ever. The negotiations were as intense as anything I've ever experienced. My lenders behaved honorably throughout, but the press consistently got the story wrong, exaggerating the likelihood of my demise— and hoping for it. I see the deal as a great victory— and eventually the rest of the world will too. Sure it was nerve-racking when everybody was watching and wondering if I'd fail. I couldn't speak out without endangering the negotiations. Still, in the midst of it all, I realized that I was doing what I love to do most—battle back from the brink.

There is no question that the early nineties will be, for me and many other entrepreneurs, a period of retrenchment, a time when the businessmen who made it big in the eighties will have to get leaner and meaner again and lose some of those helicopters, private jets, and other expensive toys. But I also see these next few years as a period of great opportunity—in some ways very similar to the time when I got started fifteen years ago.

One of the main things I know now that I didn't know then, or even a couple of years ago, has to do with invincibility. Let me tell you what I mean:

It was a Sunday afternoon in Tokyo, and I was feeling impatient and still a little strung out from jet lag. In a few minutes Mike Tyson would be fighting James "Buster" Douglas.

Usually I enjoy the spectacle of a major heavyweight fight, especially when it involves Iron Mike, a fighter I've come to know and respect. But Tyson had such an aura of invincibility at that point—February of 1990—that the outcome of the fight seemed like a foregone conclusion, and I just wished it were over with. I'd already been in Japan several days, working on a few possible business deals. I'd signed a lot of autographs, and I'd been deeply impressed with the Japanese passion for precision in everything they do. But now I wanted nothing more than to be back in New York.

I wasn't the only one who thought the fight was a waste of time. The bookmakers were refusing to take bets on Tyson at any odds. The huge arena was about one-third empty because the Japanese people, who are no fools, assumed this was going to be another one- or two-round massacre. And even Mike himself seemed to be looking beyond Buster Douglas. A couple of nights before the fight, I had heard him tell one of my business associates—a woman who had just wished him good luck against Douglas—"Don't worry, baby, I know how to take care of business."

In retrospect I realize I should have known, when I saw Mike believing his own braggadocio, that he was due for a fall. But I could never have predicted that it would come as soon as it did. What happened after the bell rang has, of course, gone down in boxing history as one of the greatest upsets of all time. I remember that after about three rounds of watching Douglas beat up relentlessly on Mike, I turned to Don King, who was seated near me, and said, "What the hell is going on here?"

"I don't know," said Don. "I just don't know."

Then came rounds four, five, and six. Mike, who had never lost or even come close to losing, continued to get hammered. Finally Don King turned to me, shook his head, and said, "Unbelievable, man. Really unbelievable."

He was certainly right about that. There was a brief moment in the eighth round when, you may recall, Mike rallied and knocked down Douglas, who seemed to benefit from a long count—an impression that was confirmed by the videotape. But the tape also showed that Mike was getting his ass whipped for ten solid rounds before he finally fell. In the end, that's all that mattered.

Some people say Mike lost on purpose, to set up a big-money rematch with Douglas. That's nonsense. What most people don't know—and what I myself found out only later—is that Mike was so sure of winning against Douglas that he did not even have an automatic rematch clause in his contract. Besides, Mike would never do anything—especially give up his championship belt—solely for the money involved. At twenty-three he had already learned the important truth that money in itself is not a very interesting commodity.

What *is* fascinating, to me at least, is the game we all play to get whatever money and status we have. That's why, as I watched the former champ being helped to his feet and saw the sportswriters running to the interview room so they could ask, ''What happened, Mike?'' I realized something.

The key question now is really: What happens to Mike Tyson *from this point on*?—because for him the game has changed. As a matter of fact, after a four-month layoff, Mike won his next fight decisively.

But against Douglas, Mike learned something about himself, and about life. And now he has to go into the world every day with the knowledge that, though he may be a great fighter, he is not all-powerful. There are some aspects of his life over which he has no control.

I didn't know that at twenty-three. But I can identify with that now.

It's not that I've suffered a knockout blow. Far from it. But after a long winning streak I'm being tested under pressure. I've also been in the public eye long enough so that the pendulum has swung, and many of the same media people who once put me on a pedestal now can't wait for me to fall off. People like a hero, a Golden Boy, but many like a fallen hero even better. That was a fact of life long before I came along, and I can handle it. I know that, whatever happens, I'm a survivor—a survivor of success, which is a very rare thing indeed.

The basic process of growth and change that I'm describing is not something unique to Donald Trump. It happens to everybody who is lucky enough not to die young. The main difference between me and others is that I've had to face my challenges and make my tough decisions under the glare of a white-hot spotlight. I'm not complaining about the attention I get. Publicity is important because it creates interest in my hotels, residential buildings, and other projects. But sometimes it gets out of hand, and my every move is scrutinized by the press to the point of absurdity.

To cite one example, I'm obviously not the only

guy in his forties who has separated from his wife. Yet I may be the first who's had to endure many months of sleazy headlines and news broadcasts about the breakup—and TV shows filled with therapists and lawyers I've never met babbling about my supposed marital problems as if they knew what they were talking about.

The publicity gradually dehumanizes you. To many people, Donald Trump isn't a flesh-and-blood human being anymore. Instead, I'm a symbol—of wealth, fame, egotism, greed, and probably several other not-so-nice things. My estrangement from my wife, Ivana, isn't seen as a sad occurrence, like the breakup of other families. Instead, it's a melodrama played up for other people's entertainment. Members of the media, some of whom I've known for many years, call me for information, as I suppose they must when editors tell them to. But when I cooperate and try to explain my position, they write that "publicity is Trump's cocaine."

Reality never seems to get in anyone's way. Never mind, for example, that I have a solid relationship with my children; people—often the same people who print headlines that could cause my kids so much confusion and embarrassment if they weren't sheltered from them—will criticize me as a father. And it doesn't seem to matter that my buildings in New York and my casino-hotels in Atlantic City are doing well despite generally bad market conditions. Some writers and broadcasters will continue to say that I'm about to fall or have already collapsed.

Look, I don't expect anyone to feel sorry for me, but the fact is, I'm only human. Furthermore, the Trump Organization is in some ways like the Disney Company: Image means a great deal to me. If people don't associate my name with quality and success, I've got serious problems. So do the thousands of people who work for me and depend for their livelihood on my doing well. Unfortunately, years of relentless striving for perfection go into creating an image, but just a few potshots from some jerks with word processors can tarnish a reputation.

But it's not just the business press—and the public's desire to see the mighty fall—that makes life in the so-called fast lane so dangerous and, for many, so temporary as well. Anyone who makes it to the top of his profession will tell you, if he's honest, that his worst potential enemy is himself. It's a rare person who can achieve a major goal in life and not almost immediately start feeling sad, empty, and a little lost. If you look at the record—which in this case means newspapers, magazines, and TV news—you'll see that an awful lot of people who achieve success, from Elvis Presley to Ivan Boesky, lose their direction or their ethics.

Actually, I don't have to look at anyone else's life to know that's true. I'm as susceptible to that pitfall as anyone else.

A very good friend—Alan Greenberg, the head of the Wall Street investment firm of Bear Stearns—tells me that I suffer from what he jokingly refers to as the "Is That All There Is?" syndrome. This came up when we were talking one day about my yacht, the *Trump Princess*, which is generally considered the most luxurious private yacht in the world.

"You know," I said to Alan, "I'm thinking of selling my boat and, with the profit I make, building another that would be almost twice as big. What do you think of the idea?"

"I think it sounds like classic Donald Trump," he said.

"Oh?" I said. "And what does that mean?"

"It means," he said, "that, for you, getting there isn't half the fun, it's almost all the fun. You set out to achieve something, you get what you are after, and then you immediately start singing that old Peggy Lee song 'Is That All There Is?' "

Alan was right about that. If you have a striving personality, the challenge matters most, not the reward. The truth is, almost nothing in life is what it's cracked up to be—except perhaps the battle to get where you want to go.

A lot of people who've made it big never realize that. They get to the top of their profession, be it show business or real estate or Wall Street, and then they wonder why they don't feel fulfilled. They get confused, they get depressed. They take drugs, they self-destruct. It's become a sad cliché.

Chris Evert stands out to me as a shining example of how self-awareness can prevent self-destruction. I remember that when she retired from tennis in 1989, she didn't talk primarily about the game passing her by, or wanting to settle down and have babies. Rather, what she said first was that she had finally realized that the brief thrill of holding the Wimbledon or U.S. Open trophy above her head and twirling around for the photographers was no longer worth the tremendous effort it took to get to that point. Instead of trying to figure out why that was so, she just accepted the fact that she didn't really "have it made," as she once thought she would if she could only win those prizes. And then Chris Evert, wisely and without regrets, moved on to face new challenges with a wonderful new husband, Andy Mill.

To be always moving toward a new goal—if that's not the key to happiness, then it's the key to achieving a state that's as close to happiness as you're going to get in this life.

I can honestly say that I've never suffered through a prolonged period of depression. That may have something to do with genes—or with my life-style, which is free of unnatural highs and thus the unnatural lows that always follow them. Yet I believe I've also been helped by the realization that life is a series of struggles. And there's nothing I or anyone else can do about that. In fact, I've come to relish the struggles.

I was up at West Point not long ago, strolling the grounds while talking with some military men. At one point we found ourselves standing before a statue of General Douglas MacArthur, and I couldn't help but be struck by the inscription, which was taken from a speech he'd made at the Academy while receiving the Sylvanus Thayer Award in 1962.

"Your mission remains fixed, determined, inviolable," he said. "It is to win our wars. Everything else in your professional career is but corollary to this vital dedication. All other public purposes, all other public projects, all other public needs, great or small, will find others for their accomplishment. . . ."

Just win wars. The general was talking to soldiers, of course, but I felt that what he said applied to me as well. My main purpose in life is to keep winning. And the reason for that is simple: If I don't win, I don't get to fight the next battle.

At the same time, there are no guarantees in this world.

Even if you do keep winning, it could all be over, suddenly, at any time. That truth really hit home on the morning of October 10, 1989. I know the date because it was a day that changed my life.

It started out in the most ordinary fashion. I remember looking out from my apartment on the sixty-

helped first in Las Vegas and later in Atlantic City. Mark had grown up at Grossinger's, the famous Catskills resort that his family had owned, and from there had gone on to distinguish himself at the Golden Nugget, just down the Atlantic City Boardwalk from my properties. Jon, a Cornell graduate, had worked at the Hilton in Philadelphia.

Besides being great executives, those guys were just plain good people—three of the happiest, most well-adjusted men I've ever met. Steve, forty-three, was a devout Mormon—a heavyset, homespun kind of guy who was extremely active in community affairs. Born and raised in Utah, Steve had a lovely wife, Donna, and eight children. He was easy to talk to and knew as much about me and my innermost thoughts as anyone did. Often when I was down in Atlantic City, I'd settle into one of the deep leather couches in Steve's office at Trump Castle for a conversation that might touch on everything from last night's slot-machine drop to what I should do next with my life. Steve shared a trait with virtually everyone who is successful in dealing with other people: He knew how to listen.

Mark was also a family man, devoted to his wonderful wife, Lauren, and their two beautiful children, Scott and Rachel, and active in all sorts of local charities. Because he was about five years younger than I, I thought of Mark as something of a kid brother—but one whose instincts about the hotel business I respected immensely. Even at golf, Mark was of championship caliber. He had the gift of getting along with people effortlessly, be they construction workers, businessmen booking a convention at one of our places, or big-time gamblers. He could charm even a shrewd operator like Don King—which is why I put Mark in charge of my boxing operations in Atlantic City.

As for Jon, he was probably the most promising hotel executive I'd ever come across. Although his background was primarily in the financial end of the business, he was quickly becoming what one of my senior executives called our "personality guy" on the property: the kind of young man who could walk through the casino and greet all of the employees— and many of our regular and most valued customers —by their first names. He was also a great athlete who had played baseball in college and starred on the Trump team that played in the Atlantic City hotel league in the summer. Jon was engaged to another Trump Plaza employee, Beth McFadden, and they planned to be married sometime in 1990.

During that October 10 press conference, Mark was, as usual, overflowing with enthusiasm, not just about the fight we were promoting that day but also about the progress of the Taj Mahal in general, and even about the amusement park we were planning to build on a steel pier that projected into the ocean. "I can't wait to bring back the rides," I remember his saying to some reporters that morning. "The family aspect of Atlantic City has been lost for much too long. It'll be great when we finally get it going again."

And it will, although Mark won't be there to see it.

It's not fair, but so much of life comes down to chance. In my first book I wrote about an incident when a huge crane fell on a precast-concrete parking garage, causing the whole structure to collapse. About one hundred men had left the site just moments before, and so, despite the spectacular mishap, no one was even slightly injured. This time, luck was running the other way.

The press conference ended, and I went back to my office with my three friends for a brief meeting. We talked for an hour or so about how well we were doing and about the progress of construction on the Taj Mahal, which at that time was about six months from completion. Then Steve, who was one of the hardest-working guys I ever met, said, "Donald, we've got to run now. We've got to catch a helicopter."

I very casually looked up and said, "I'll see you guys over the weekend."

For an instant, as they were walking out, I thought of going with them. I fly down to Atlantic City at least once a week, and I knew that if I made the forty-five-minute helicopter trip then, we could continue talking business on the way. But there was just too much to do in the office that day. As quickly as the idea had popped into my mind, I decided not to go. Instead, I just said good-bye and went back to reading reports and making phone calls.

About an hour and a half later, I got a call from Steve Hyde's secretary of fifteen years, Jeri Haase. She was asking where Steve, Mark, and Jon were. A car was waiting for them at Bader Field in Atlantic City, she said, and the driver had just called to say they hadn't arrived on schedule.

I didn't think very much about that call. There are two airports in Atlantic City, and I figured there had probably been some kind of mix-up and the problem would get straightened out in short order. About ten minutes later, though, Jeri called again, saying that the company from which their helicopter had been leased, Paramount Aviation, had called her to say that the helicopter was down, but that they had no other facts. At that point I started to get a little worried, but I still wasn't overly concerned. I'd heard of helicopters landing for repairs, or just to check on something for safety's sake, and I thought that this was probably one of those cases.

But it wasn't. The next call came from CBS-TV news, about five minutes later. Now I was worried, and before the reporter could ask me any questions, I asked him if he'd heard anything from the state police. He responded in a cold voice, as if he'd seen it all before.

"Five dead, Mr. Trump," he said flatly. "Do you have any comment?"

"What?" I asked.

"Five dead," he repeated. "All in body bags. Any comment?"

I don't remember exactly what I said to him before hanging up. After that, the calls came in quickly, and we learned some details. The helicopter had gone down on the Garden State Parkway. The pilot and copilot, both Paramount Aviation employees, had also been killed in the crash, along with Jon, Mark, and Steve.

My first thoughts were for the families that had been left behind. I also couldn't help imagining what my friends' final seconds must have been like, and hoping that they had suffered as little as possible. During the next few days, as I attended the funeral services of Steve, Mark, and Jon, I felt sadder than I've ever felt in my life—and at times extremely angry, too. (In one of the dozens of stories about me that ran in the late spring, a reporter made it sound as if I were criticizing the three for their work at the casinos. Let me set the record straight once and for all. They were terrific.)

The helicopter those men were on should never have been allowed to fly. As it turned out, the rotors had split apart in midair.

We are now in court with Agusta, the aircraft's Italian manufacturer, and we expect to make them pay dearly. But, of course, no matter how much we win, Steve, Mark, Jon, and the two helicopter pilots are gone. That tragedy will always be a waste of five young lives.

But after thinking about it long and hard, I believe there is, at least, one valuable truth to be salvaged from the deaths of Steve, Mark, and Jon.

Life is fragile. It doesn't matter who you are, how good you are at what you do, how many beautiful buildings you put up, or how many people know your name. No one on earth can be totally secure, because nothing can completely protect you from life's tragedies and the relentless passage of time.

In some ways, the Trump Organization has adjusted to the tragedy of October 10, 1989. Ed Tracy now heads up my Atlantic City operations, and Bucky Howard has assumed the top spot at the Taj. Mitchell Etess, Mark's brother, has been appointed to a position similar to that once held by Jon Benanav.

Life in Atlantic City, and elsewhere, will go on. But I know we will never adjust completely to the loss we suffered. I'd like everyone in my organization to remember that there were once men named Steve Hyde, Mark Etess, and Jon Benanav who worked there—and that they were great, and ultimately showed us how fragile life really is.

TWO

THE
SURVIVAL
GAME

THE most amazing things come my way each day in the mail, over the fax machine, and via messenger. I'm talking about bouquets of roses and lawsuits; marriage proposals and offers to invest in Florida swampland; cheesecakes and stuffed skunks. Not long ago, one of my secretaries opened an envelope and found a story, typed neatly on a piece of plain white paper. It really made me think.

In 1923 eight of the world's greatest financiers met in Chicago. The group included the president of the largest gas company, the greatest wheat speculator, a member of the President's cabinet, the greatest bear on Wall Street, the head of the world's greatest monopoly, and the president of the Bank of International Settlement.

These would certainly be considered among the world's most successful men. At least they had found the secret to making money. But now, more than sixty years later, where are these men?

The president of the largest independent steel company, Charles Schwab, died a pauper. The last few years of his life he lived on borrowed money.

The president of the largest gas company, Howard Hobson, went insane.

The greatest wheat speculator, Arthur Colton, died abroad, insolvent.

The president of the New York Stock Exchange, Richard Whitney, served time in Sing Sing Prison.

The member of the President's cabinet, Alfred Fall, was pardoned and released from prison so he could die at home.

The greatest bear on Wall Street, Jesse Livermore, died a suicide.

The head of the world's greatest monopoly, Ivor Kruger, the Match King, died a suicide.

The president of the Bank of International Settlement shot himself.

Quite a fun bunch, no? And yet very typical. The moral of that sad tale is that success is far more difficult to maintain than it is to achieve.

If you doubt that, you've never been successful. Let

me make this absolutely clear: This chapter is not a whine. Everyone knows the benefits of wealth and fame—for instance, that I can, in theory, go anywhere and do anything I want. The trouble is, in reality life at the top comes with very little freedom. I can't walk down Fifth Avenue anymore without being mobbed. I can't go to the movies without sending two body-guards to hold my seats until the lights go out and I can slip in quietly. And the simple pleasure of attend-ing the U.S. Open tennis tournament in Flushing Meadows and just sitting back and watching the profes-sionals play their game—that's probably lost to me forever.

Of course, much worse problems can come with being famous—ask Ethel Kennedy or Jackie Onassis. And even those who survive physically often become mentally and emotionally crippled by success.

Consider, for example, the career of Howard Hughes. Hughes stands out as perhaps the classic ex-ample of someone who was victimized by his own fame and fortune. To many people today he symbolizes weirdness; he is probably doomed to be remembered as the guy with the long fingernails and the wild hair.

That's a shame, because here was a guy who at one time was movie-star handsome, a certified billionaire, and a genius in several fields. Hughes had it all, and judging by the number of beautiful ex-girlfriends who are still writing books about him, he seemed, for a while at least, to be living life to the hilt. Yet the pressure of being a larger-than-life figure was apparently so mind-boggling that it gradually drove him crazy. Hughes—the man who revolutionized Las Vegas by bringing a corporate approach to what had been a mob-dominated business—eventually became unwilling to venture out of his own penthouse. He degenerated into a totally reclusive creature who, toward the end of his life, refused even to defend himself from worthless lawsuits filed against him.

The Howard Hughes story is fascinating to me because it shows that it's possible to fall very far very fast. As time goes on I find myself thinking more and more about Howard Hughes and even, to some degree, identifying with him. Take, for example, his famous aversion to germs. While I'm certainly not as fanatical as he was, I've always had very strong feelings about cleanliness. I'm constantly washing my hands, and it wouldn't bother me if I never had to shake hands with a well-meaning stranger again. Yet because of the life I lead and the need to visit my various properties, I'm often put in an uncomfortable position. Whenever I'm in Atlantic City, casino customers come up and touch me for good luck, and there are times when I'm approached in restaurants by nice people who nevertheless don't seem to notice that they are spraying their good wishes all over my food.

Every time that happens, Howard Hughes and his reclusive life-style look a little less crazy to me.

Hughes was deeply involved with drugs, of course.

But drugs, I believe, are only a symptom of the problems that come with great success. From what I've seen, it's fame itself that bends people out of shape. In fact, the more celebrities I meet, the more I realize that fame is a kind of drug, one that is way too powerful for most people to handle.

I'll never forget the time a few years ago when Ivana and I happened to be in Monte Carlo, and we got a call in our hotel room from Frank Sinatra. I was a little surprised because I hardly knew Sinatra, but Frank said that he was in town with his wife and asked if we would join them and another couple (the actor Roger Moore and his wife) for dinner at the very fine restaurant on top of the Hotel de Paris. I accepted.

I quickly went from being impressed to being shocked.

From the moment we sat down at the table, Sinatra seemed edgy. Then, a short way into the dinner, his wife, Barbara, said something mildly critical about Ronald Reagan. It was such an insignificant remark that I don't even remember what it was. But Sinatra exploded, using the worst language imaginable. "You piece of human garbage," he said to Barbara at one point. Then, just so the other women at the table wouldn't feel neglected, he added, "You fuckin' broads are all alike. You're the scum of the earth."

The rest of us just stared at our food and pretended this wasn't happening. All I could think to say was "So, Ivana, how's your pasta?"

By the time we reached dessert Sinatra's anger seemed to have subsided, and I thought the worst was over. But then, as we were leaving, a young couple came walking up to us. Seeing Sinatra, they were obviously both nervous and delighted to have spotted their all-time idol.

"Mr. Sinatra," the man said, "my wife and I both love you. Could I please have your autograph?"

I turned to Frank and I saw blood in his eye. "Get this bum out of here!" he screamed to one of his bodyguards, who was standing nearby. "Get this goddamn creep out of here!"

Needless to say, the poor guy and his wife were totally shattered. They walked away not quite sure what had happened to them.

The rest of us, meanwhile, got on the elevator and headed down to the lobby—but not Sinatra, who quickly reached over and pushed the button for the second floor. "I can't walk through lobbies," he mumbled. "I get mobbed."

As Sinatra stalked off the elevator and headed toward a door marked Fire Stairs, I realized that all those years of being pampered and catered to—and also pressured, stared at, and criticized—had clearly taken their toll. Despite his millions of dollars and countless loyal fans, the baggage of being a celebrity was weighing him down.

That dinner turned out to be a terribly awkward experience, but it gave me a lot to think about.

* * *

Obviously, you don't *have* to be crazy or mean just because you're successful.

Someone I admire greatly for the way he handles all the attention is Bob Hope. Bob causes a stir wherever he goes, and has for more than sixty years, but by now he's got the crowd-control part of his life down to a science. I've watched him walk through a crowded lobby, and I've noticed that he always goes as quickly as possible, signing whatever pieces of paper are thrust in front of him, but never breaking his stride. Then with a smile and a wave he's into the elevator, the doors close, and he's gone. On the way out, it's the same thing—step, sign, smile, and into the car. Everyone's happy and nobody feels neglected. And Bob gets on with his life. That's probably why he's been so successful for so long—and why he's so healthy and robust in his mid-eighties.

Other celebrities, however, always seem to be struggling to swim upstream when they're in public. Johnny Carson, for example, was finally forced to sell his apartment in Trump Tower in order to escape all the commotion he caused just by going in and out of the residential entrance. He's a huge talent but so private that it was painful to watch him trying to cope with the adoring crowds.

Actually, it's not the people with their autograph books and the outstretched hands who are the real problem for those who've achieved a certain level of fame and success. More often than not, it's the press. I know that the real danger in criticizing the media is that they will have the last word about everything I'm ever involved in, personally and professionally, including this book. Frankly, I don't care. The media didn't build Trump Tower or the Taj Mahal. The reporters aren't taking the risks. I am. And the public seems to understand that.

I should say that over the years I've found most reporters to be evenhanded and honest, even if they weren't exactly on my side in the articles and TV pieces that eventually appeared. But there are enough exceptions to that rule, especially since my separation from Ivana, to make dealing with the press a potentially frustrating and sometimes dangerous proposition.

For example, I don't know how many times I've heard the fairy tale that I got my first book on the bestseller list by buying up thousands of copies and storing them in a warehouse someplace. That's nonsense—a complete lie. To compile its list, *The New York Times* monitors sales at certain bookstores that are scattered either around the New York area or across the country—I'm not even sure which; no one outside the *Times* knows. The point is, anyone who wanted to manipulate the list would have to buy up all the books at every store he could find and just hope he had hit the right places. To do that would be impossible, and to even attempt to do it would require a burning desire to waste money and time. I did at one time purchase a few thousand books, but these were bought wholesale and virtually all were resold to customers at my Atlantic City hotels and Trump Tower.

Incidentally, many writers also referred to *The Art of the Deal* as Donald Trump's "poorly reviewed book." This also bothered me no end because the reviews were overwhelmingly positive, from *The New York Times* on down.

Another myth that's made the rounds is that I was blackballed from the Palm Beach Bath and Tennis Club in Florida. I remember turning on the *Today* show one morning and seeing some terrible woman relating with great smugness and certainty that I had applied for admission to the club (which happens to be across the street from my home in Palm Beach) and that I'd been rejected by the supposedly snooty "old money" people down there. "You know," she said, obviously delighted with herself, "that club is quite closed down to people like Donald Trump." I couldn't believe what I was hearing. Not only was her report not true, it was exactly the opposite of reality. Many of the members of that club had urged me to join, but I had declined their invitation. (The interesting part of this news report was that the woman broadcaster was Jewish and therefore would not have been allowed to visit the club, let alone become a member—one of the reservations I had about the club.)

Early in my career I was naïve about how things worked with some reporters. When a guy named Wayne Barrett called me years ago and said he was from *The Village Voice* and wanted to write a story about me, I said sure without hesitation. I knew *The Village Voice* was not exactly overloaded with Pulitzer Prize winners, nor was it one of America's most respected newspapers, yet I had been written about very little at that point, and I saw this as an opportunity to promote the Grand Hyatt Hotel, the convention center, and several other projects I was working on at the time.

I invited Barrett to my office and my apartment and talked to him openly and at great length. I was 100 percent honest with him, which was easy, since I had nothing to hide. And he sat there, acting nice as could be, asking questions, and recording everything on tape.

What could go wrong, you might think, in that kind of situation? The answer is, almost everything.

Soon afterward I showed up on the cover of the *Voice*, the subject of a vicious article in which virtually every quote had been changed or taken wildly out of context. Having the story appear was frustrating enough. But then federal prosecutors started looking into Barrett's allegations about my business practices. They soon decided this was a noncase, and the whole thing was dropped and done with before I, in my naïveté, really got a handle on exactly what was happening. In retrospect, though, I'm glad I had the experience, because I learned that as soon as you reach an even slightly prominent position in life, people will try to make a name for themselves by knocking you down. Barrett, whose last book was a major failure, is still trying to make his name at my expense. He is, I have heard, writing a book about me. The good news for me is that he's never been a writer who could capture and hold anyone's interest.

Sometimes journalistic attacks have little to do with the pursuit of truth. They are personal vendettas disguised as objective reporting. The cover story that *Forbes* magazine did on me in its May 14, 1990, issue is a case in point. HOW MUCH IS DONALD TRUMP WORTH? the headline asked. The answer, according to *Forbes*, was about $500 million—or much less than the $1.7 billion the magazine had said I was worth a year before. The story painted a portrait of me as a besieged businessman who was getting by mostly on chutzpah.

I do have plenty of chutzpah, and there was no question that my business interests, like those of almost everyone else in a bad economy, were going through a period of strain, but beyond that, the article was willfully wrong. In order to come up with a story that would sell magazines—and damage my reputation (something the Forbes family desperately wanted to do, for reasons I'll explain in a moment)—*Forbes*, in my opinion, undervalued such possessions of mine as, among others, the Plaza Hotel, the Trump Shuttle, and seventy-eight acres of land I own on Manhattan's Upper West Side. Who can say what these one-of-a-kind assets are worth until they're put on the market? Certainly not some mediocre reporter from *Forbes* named Richard Stern, though the magazine doesn't hesitate to assign specific dollar values to people's possessions and then go on from there to make statements and draw conclusions based on the meaningless numbers it's come up with.

However, *Forbes*'s biggest miscalculation came when it figured in the cost of building and operating the Taj Mahal in Atlantic City.

The story would have been damaging enough by itself, but what made matters worse was that it set off an avalanche of negative publicity. The media loved the idea that Trump was no longer a billionaire. It was after the *Forbes* article that all sorts of self-appointed experts were saying and writing that it was all over for Donald Trump, and that I was gone like the eighties. Liz Smith, a New York *Daily News* columnist who used to kiss my ass so much that it was downright embarrassing, reported viciously on anything I did or said (while always being sure to praise Ivana to the sky, which was fine with me).

It has always amazed me that people pay so much attention to *Forbes* magazine. Every year the "*Forbes* 400" comes out, and people talk about it as if it were a rigorously researched compilation of America's wealthiest people, instead of what it really is: a sloppy, highly arbitrary estimate of certain people's net worth. Often, how well you fared on that list depended greatly on the state of your personal relationship with the editor, the late Malcolm Forbes.

Malcolm Forbes and I did not have a good relationship. Even though he invited me, I didn't go to his much-ballyhooed seventieth birthday party in Morocco in 1989. At one time Malcolm and I had gotten along just fine; we chatted amiably at parties and occasionally talked on the phone. But I gradually came to see him as a hypocrite who favored those who advertised in his magazine and tried, with surprising viciousness, to punish those who didn't. I also saw a double standard in the way he lived openly as a homosexual—which he had every right to do—but expected the media and his famous friends to cover for him. Malcolm and the Forbes family no doubt sensed my coolness toward them, and for that reason, and also because I never advertised much in *Forbes* magazine, they were not great admirers of Donald Trump. In retrospect, I can see it was only a matter of time before the family started using its magazine against me.

The first glimpse I had of Malcolm's real nature came a few years ago, when I finally gave in to his wheedling and took an ad in his magazine. It was a simple black-and-white announcement saying that I had some apartments for sale in one of my New York buildings—the kind of ad you frequently find in the back. But Malcolm placed it prominently on the first right-hand page, so that you saw it as soon as you opened the cover. The day after it came out he called and asked if I was happy with the ad's placement. I naturally said I was, but to myself I was thinking that I didn't like his way of doing business. Malcolm was being a little too nice—trying to make me feel I owed *him* something. Like, for instance, another ad. Instead of getting him off my back, I was only setting myself up for more of his sales pitch, and I didn't like it.

Still, my serious problems with Malcolm didn't start until I bought Adnan Khashoggi's magnificent yacht, the *Nabila*, and rechristened it the *Trump Princess*. Malcolm, for years, had a yacht called the *Highlander*, of which he was very proud. He used the boat for parties, which he intended to be glamorous, celebrity-studded events, but which in reality were mainly occasions for him to impress prospective advertisers. Malcolm also took many writers, broadcasters, and photographers on his cruises around the harbor. As a result, he became a darling of the New York press, and his 150-foot yacht was legendary—until I came along with a much more luxurious, 282-foot yacht and stole the spotlight away.

What really ruined our relationship, though, was an incident, only a short time before Forbes died, involving a couple of his young male companions. I was working in my office late one afternoon when I got a call from one of my people at the Plaza Hotel. The man said that Malcolm wanted to bring two young men who appeared to be well under the legal drinking age into the Oak Room Bar. Normally, my staff would ask anyone who appeared to be underage to take a seat at a table if they wanted to have a club soda or a Coke. But because my executive had recognized Malcolm and knew that he and I were acquaintances, he hesitated, and decided to call me for further instructions.

I didn't have to think about the matter for very long.

"Please nicely convince Mr. Forbes that it would be better for him to go to another room, such as the Palm Court," I said. There was not much reason for debate, as I saw it, because we were talking about compliance with the state liquor laws.

Malcolm, however, was outraged that he hadn't received special treatment. The next day he called and screamed at me, saying that I'd treated him shabbily, embarrassed him publicly—and that he would get even with me. Perhaps my guy could have been more of a diplomat, but I'm certain I did the right thing.

It was only a few weeks later that I got word that *Forbes* magazine was planning a cover story on me, and that one of the reporters assigned to the project was a man named Richard Stern. A couple of years before, Stern had written an article about my Resorts International deal with Merv Griffin. That piece was highly inaccurate and was based on the premise that Merv had gotten the better of me. When time proved

Stern wrong, and Merv filed for Chapter 11 protection, Malcolm claimed to be mortified by the story and apologized to me for it on more than one occasion. But now I was once again faced with Richard Stern, a reporter with a proven anti-Trump bias. (His coauthor, John J. Connolly, was fired by Forbes a few weeks later, when it was disclosed he had violated ethical standards on several occasions. Stern himself was accused in a Wall Street newsletter of improprieties.)

When that *Forbes* cover story on me ran, I looked at the unfair estimates of my assets and the omitted income from the Taj Mahal and shook my head. This wasn't journalism, I thought to myself, this was Malcolm finally getting back at me from the grave, with the help of his family, especially his son Steve.

(Some people even began saying that I had engineered the *Forbes* story as a means of negotiating a better divorce settlement with Ivana. Come to think of it, that wouldn't have been a bad move.)

Being the cover subject for *Time* magazine—although it sounds in some ways like the ultimate evidence that you've arrived in the world—was an almost equally sleazy experience.

I'll never forget how the process started. I got a call one day in 1988 from a reporter at *Time*, asking if I minded if they did a cover story on me. Right away, it struck me as odd that they asked my permission. What kind of aggressive news organization, I wondered, would give a subject the option of being written about? But I kept that question to myself and said, "If that's what you want, go ahead." Despite my initial qualms, it did seem to me something of an honor to be profiled in a *Time* cover story at this early stage of my life.

The *Time* reporter who eventually showed up to interview me was a woman who obviously thought she was something of a man-killer in more ways than one. While I sat there in a state of disbelief, this very ordinary woman sauntered into my office like Marilyn Monroe, sat herself down, and immediately launched into a story about a messy divorce she was going through. Speaking of her estranged husband, she said, as I recall, something like "I'm going to rip his heart out by the time I'm finished." She had a smile on her face as she spoke, but this was clearly a woman seething with hostility. All I could think, as I smiled back, was Oh, great, I'm going to be written about in *Time* by a woman who rips men's hearts out.

As it turned out, she wasn't the writer. *Time* has a ridiculous system whereby certain people go out and do the interviewing, and then the story gets written by someone back in the office who never even meets the people he or she is writing about. To me, this makes no sense whatsoever. I can see doing it that way if you're covering a breaking story in, say, the Far East, or if you're reporting a trend in various places across America. But this was a profile of one person, and the Time & Life Building is about a ten-minute walk from Trump Tower. Why the writer couldn't come over to meet me during the several months it took *Time* to put the story together is something I'll never understand.

In any case, the reporter certainly had energy to burn. Jeannie McDowell hung around me constantly, in New York and Atlantic City, and when she wasn't with me, she was off trying to track down everyone I'd shaken hands with in the past thirty years. Reporters who've interviewed me know I'm from the "anything goes" school. I have nothing to hide, and no questions are off-limits as far as I'm concerned. I also believed at the time that it was always best to give an interview, rather than making yourself unavailable, because that way you at least have some chance of getting your message across. (I no longer believe this. I've been burned too many times by reporters who have a point to make and will make it—at my expense—no matter what I say.)

Still, I often felt wary when I spoke to McDowell. There was something about the tone of her questions that struck me as strange. Instead of eliciting information, she often seemed determined to stir up trouble for reasons that, as far as I could see, had nothing whatsoever to do with her article.

Her associate operated the same way. One day she

showed up at the office of my sister Maryanne, who is a federal judge in New Jersey. "How does it feel," she asked Maryanne, "to be earning the salary of a federal employee while your brother lives in mansions?" Now, my sister, as it happens, has nothing to apologize for. Before her son was born she earned a master's degree in public law and government. When David entered the sixth grade she went to law school, and today she is one of the most respected federal judges in the country. Maryanne, in her way, explained this to the reporter. "Well, Donald has his life, and I have mine, and there are no problems between us," she said. But the *Time* woman was relentless. "So, how does it feel to fly Eastern when your brother has his own private plane?" she asked Maryanne, going back over the same ground, and always with a sort of sneer. What she was doing, it seemed to Maryanne and later to me, was trying to drive a wedge between family members, though for what purpose God only knows.

While the *Time* reporters were screwing around conducting interviews of that kind, I got a call from a man named Robert Miller. I'd never heard of him before, but he said he was the publisher of *Time* and congratulated me on being chosen as a cover subject. He then went on to say that because I was going to be on the cover, he would like to hold a party in my honor at Le Cirque, one of New York's finest restaurants.

There would be maybe a hundred people there, he said, and he asked if, during the course of the party, I might get up and speak to the assembled guests.

Like several other things I'd heard from *Time* people, this didn't sound quite right. In the first place, I don't like parties and the small talk and the standing around that go with them. And I don't relish giving speeches at eleven in the evening. But in this case there was something about having a party for the subject of a not-yet-published profile that, in my opinion, didn't jibe with objective journalism.

"Tell me," I said to Mr. Miller, "did you have a party for Qaddafi when you put him on the cover? Did you go to Le Cirque with the Ayatollah? Look," I went on, "if you're going to do a cover story, do a cover story; if not, you can forget the whole thing. But you don't have to honor me."

He was insistent, though. "Please, Donald," he said. "This is something we do with our cover people, and we've invited various dignitaries from around New York, leaders in the fields of business, politics, and education, so why don't you be there?"

I guess I was impressed enough with *Time*'s reputation, despite my experiences with its people, so that I relented and agreed to show up. I should have followed my gut instinct. I barely had one foot in the door of Le Cirque when Miller grabbed me and said, "I'd like you to meet the head of the Buick division of General Motors." And then, "Donald, say hello to the head of Volvo of America." Next it was "Please meet Mr. Colgate-Palmolive."

After one or two more introductions it was clear to me what was happening, and I took Miller aside. I was calm but firm. "I see the real purpose of this thing is to set me up with your advertisers," I said. "Well, I can understand your wanting to do that, and I certainly wouldn't rule out speaking to them. But you should tell me what I'm here for, and not tell me this is just to honor me for being on the cover of *Time*."

Miller was full of apologies and explanations. I think he was afraid I would walk out. Instead of creating a scene, though, I stayed—and wound up giving my speech. Some nights you're on and some you aren't; that evening, despite the aggravating circumstances, everything fell into place, and by the time I finished taking the audience's many questions it was about midnight.

Because things worked out so well, I was able to extract my revenge later. What happened was that some *Newsweek* editors heard about the dinner—and the *Time* story—and immediately called me to set up a series of interviews. A couple of weeks later, while *Time* was still dithering around, *Newsweek* came out with its cover story on me.

Not everything in the piece was flattering or positive, but I must admit the story was interesting, basically accurate, and quite fair. I was glad I'd taken the time to sit for interviews with its writers, Bill

Powell and Peter McKillop. They, unlike the *Time* reporters, seemed prepared to plow ahead whether I cooperated or not. I know *Newsweek* was pleased with the story too.

The *Time* story finally appeared some months later—shortly after the sales figures came back showing that the *Newsweek* cover story had been a huge hit, one of their best-selling issues of the past several years. (My strength at the newsstands was a double-edged sword. The minute I got into some trouble, *Newsweek*—with its advertising on the skids—jumped on the bandwagon and put me back on the cover with the nastiest piece of all.)

When I read what *Time* published, I could only shake my head in disbelief. I should say now that since the time of this incident, I've developed a great respect for some of the top executives at what is now Time Warner. But the cover story that finally came out, while hardly the worst piece ever written about me, was snide, sloppy, and inaccurate—a very tired piece of writing that had the feel of something slapped together at the last minute, despite their many months of lead time. Jeannie McDowell was, as I had thought, a true disaster.

Still, it was *Time* magazine, and when my picture appeared on the cover, people called me to offer their congratulations, and to ask me how it felt to receive this honor.

"Oh, it feels fine," I told the callers, just to be polite.

The truth was that it didn't feel like much of anything. There I was, looking out from every newsstand in America, and holding an ace of diamonds in my hand. But in my mind all I could hear, once again, was Peggy Lee singing "Is That All There Is?"

The press, unfortunately, is only one of the elements I have to deal with.

What bothers me equally is the way the criminal justice system encourages the worst sorts of lowlifes to sling mud for their own protection. The more prominent your name, the more tempting a target you make for some character trying to plea-bargain or gain immunity. All some convicted felon has to do is to say the words "Donald Trump," or name some other celebrity, and certain law enforcement officials, and reporters, start dreaming of a case or a story that will make their careers.

Some time ago government agents came to my office to talk about a guy I knew only by reputation. "Is it true, Mr. Trump," they asked me, "that on a certain date, three years ago, you met this man on Fifth Avenue?"

My first reaction was to say no, because I didn't think I had. But then I vaguely remembered that this person had in fact come up to me on Fifth Avenue one day years before, shouting, "Donald Trump, Donald Trump, how are you?"

"Yes, now that you mention it, I do remember his coming up to me," I told the agents.

"And did you discuss such-and-such a deal at that time?" they asked. "And did you say *this* and did he say *that*?"

Apparently, this guy had fabricated a detailed conversation that implicated me in some scheme. All that had happened in reality was that this man had walked over, shaken my hand, and moved on. I hadn't seen him before and I haven't since.

I told that to the agents, who were real pros, and they could see I was being truthful. "No problem. We just had to follow up on it for the sake of conducting a thorough investigation," they said. "We hear this kind of stuff from these con artists all the time, and we assume ninety-nine percent of it is self-serving garbage."

That's good to know. On the other hand, it's not terribly comforting to realize that professional liars are always taking shots at you, and your fate is often in the hands of a federal or state official.

Fortunately, I've always been blessed with a kind of intuition about people that allows me to sense who the sleazy guys are, and I stay far away from them. For example, before he was convicted and sentenced to prison for insider-trading violations, Ivan Boesky and his wife came to me about renting office space in Trump Tower. Just talking to Boesky I got a funny feeling about his character, or rather his lack of it, and I told him that I was sorry but I had no office space.

It's great to have good natural instincts, but even if you do, you may find that's not enough. Over the years I've come up with certain rules for myself that are important—and in some cases vital—for surviving the perils of success.

The first and most important of these is **be disciplined**.

Discipline is something I learned from watching my father, Fred Trump—the kind of man who stays the course during good times and bad. It's the key to staying on top. It means you go to work each morning (as my father still does), and you consistently do the things that you know will get results. You push forward, then you push forward some more, and you never let your adversaries see you worried. Long vacations, drinking, drugs—all of those things are bad for discipline because they interrupt your momentum.

And momentum, when you think about it, is what surviving at the top is all about.

* * *

My next rule is **be honest**—even if the world around you is often dishonest.

Despite a brash and occasionally arrogant approach, I go by the book. I try to dot every *i* and cross every *t* when it comes to dealing with the New York City Planning Commission, the New Jersey Casino Control Commission, the SEC, or the IRS. I may be the head of a large organization, but if a government agency announces that it's come out with a new form, I'll probably stop what I'm doing and ask people to start filling it out in triplicate.

I do this because I'm an orderly person by nature and because I was raised always to do the right thing. But even if that weren't the case, there are practical reasons for me to remain honest. At this point, no amount of money I could gain by cheating could justify the risk of losing everything I've worked for in my career. My name and my reputation are very important to me.

What it comes down to is being incredibly vigilant. If a low-level accountant in my organization makes an improper adjustment to the books, either out of ignorance or because he or she is being overly aggressive, I'm the one who will have to deal with the headline that reads DONALD TRUMP COMMITS FRAUD. If a contractor I've hired violates some law or creates an unnecessary disturbance while working on a construction project, the eleven o'clock news will want a sound bite of me being interviewed about "trouble at a Trump building."

One way I keep close tabs on things is to personally sign many of the checks the Trump Organization issues. Obviously, that is a very time-consuming task, since there are thousands of checks that have to go out each week. It's also a somewhat risky practice from a legal standpoint because by demonstrating my personal involvement in every aspect of my organization, I'm forgoing what some businessmen would call insulation—that is, the ability to claim, if something goes wrong, that I didn't know what was going on. Still, my record over the years makes me certain that all those hundreds of blue felt-tip pens I've worn out signing checks have not been wasted.

Rule Three is **don't think you're so smart that you can go it alone**.

I've got a big ego. Every successful person does. At the same time, I realize that the number of calls, letters, gifts, and offers I receive daily has become almost overwhelming in the last few years. What was once a small family business has grown into a multibillion-dollar organization.

Although I am involved to some degree in virtually every aspect of my business, I couldn't be a one-man show if I wanted to, or at least I couldn't survive very long that way. So I surround myself with good people, and then I give myself the luxury of trusting them. By "good" I mean not just competent but also possessing character and class.

Nothing would be done in my office if it weren't for Norma Foerderer, my executive assistant. Norma, who has been with me practically from the beginning, worked for quite a while with the U.S. Foreign Service in Uganda and Tunisia. She does an unbelievable job of dealing with the mail and the phones—filtering out the crazy and merely strange inquiries, allowing the more interesting calls and letters to get through. I wish everyone who has asked me what my life's really like could spend a half hour or so sitting next to Norma's perpetually cluttered desk and watching her field requests. In terms of fancy footwork, she's the best.

Which leads me to my fourth rule: Although you run the risk of wasting a lot of time, **be reachable**.

I get so many letters and packages each day that my outer office sometimes looks like the General Post Office. I know celebrities who turn everything over to a fan-mail service that does nothing but send off eight-by-ten glossy photographs and form letters. I don't have that luxury because, for one thing, as a businessman, the mail is important to me. The deal for my yacht, the *Trump Princess*, began with a letter I received out of the blue from a broker of fine-quality boats in London. And not long ago one of Japan's leading developers wrote to me suggesting a plan to build a Trump Tower of the Far East and offering many millions of dollars just for the use of the name. I'm sure both those people would have been baffled to receive a smiling headshot of me and a "Dear Fan" letter in response to their inquiries. Ultimately, though, the main reason I don't ignore the letter writers is that the vast majority of them are nice people, and they deserve a considerate response.

So do the TV talk-show bookers and the people who contact me about speaking before various groups. This is another area where, as the demand for my time has increased, I've relied heavily on Norma. Although she spends long days and many evenings in the office, Norma has a great sense of which TV interview shows are hot and which others, while they may not appeal to a mass audience, are nevertheless prestigious and well worth my time. She also understands that there are certain groups and organizations about which I feel very strongly and for whom I'd readily change my schedule. If I were forced to make a choice, for example, I'd address a meeting of fifty FBI agents or Vietnam veterans rather than do a TV show that will be seen by fifty million people.

Rule Five is **stay close to home**.

It's a simple truth but a very valuable one to recognize that the world doesn't suddenly change when you're successful. What got you to the top is usually what will keep you there, and very few people have made it big without going in every day and putting in the hours. In general, my philosophy is to stay as close to home as possible. Travel is time-consuming and, in my opinion, boring—especially compared with the fun I have doing deals in my office. I can never understand people who say that if they had a lot of money they would spend their time traveling. It's just not my thing.

I did recently visit Brazil. Some key people in my organization talked me into taking a trip there to check out some possible investments and to preside over a day of horse racing sponsored by the Trump Plaza Hotel at the Jockey Club in Rio de Janeiro. I didn't particularly want to go, but there are some wealthy people in Brazil who have become friends and valued customers of my Atlantic City casinos, and my casino executives knew that it would be good for me to keep in touch with them. As in every kind of relationship, personal contact often makes all the difference.

I found Brazil to be a lovely, if economically troubled, country. And I was surprised and delighted that children came running up to me with pencils and paper yelling, ''Mr. Trump, Mr. Trump.'' My first book was a best-seller down there, and the reception I got couldn't have been warmer. But nonetheless, the experience was what my late friend Steve Hyde used to call a typical Trump trip. Which means that I left New York on Friday and flew back in time to be in the office Monday morning.

Finally, **be flexible**.

I talk a lot about dealmaking as an art, but scheduling is a minor art form in itself, especially when you're being pulled in many different directions. What Norma and I both understand is that when it comes to planning my day, there is a huge difference between working hard and being a crazed workaholic. I work from morning until night, but I try to make sure that there is plenty of white space on my appointment calendar. As Samuel Butler, the English writer, said, "To do great work a man must be very idle as well as very industrious." Those empty slots in my schedule don't represent wasted time. Not being booked solid allows me to come up with ideas rather than simply react to other people's problems. Having open time also gives me the flexibility to deal with what's really happening that day. That means that I'm rarely, if ever, in a situation where I'm, say, chatting with the prime minister of Bhutan, then posing for the cover of *Playboy*, while what I really should be doing is addressing problems at the Plaza Hotel. That may sound simple, but making sure that I run my day instead of allowing my day to run *me* is a key way I avoid being overwhelmed by work.

THREE

TRUMP VS. TRUMP

Undoing the Deal

THE newspapers called it "Trouble in Paradise."
Well, they got the first part right.

I was on my Tokyo trip when the story of my breakup with Ivana hit the streets of New York, but I could feel the heat halfway round the world. There were calls, there were inquiries, there were messages from friends warning me of true media madness.

If I had only known how crazy it was going to get, I might have stayed in Japan.

Initially, my attitude toward the separation was one of mixed emotions.

I actually welcomed it on one level. My marriage had not been working out, and perhaps this was my fault, but looking back, I believe our breakup was inevitable. Now that the other shoe was finally dropping, I had a feeling of relief. I would go back to my apartment, get whatever things I needed, and move into another apartment in Trump Tower, so near yet so totally far away.

Why had I hung in there so long when things were just not what they should have been?

That's a good question, because it's very uncharacteristic of me to act that way; I'm not one to let problems fester. My marriage, it seemed, was the only area of my life in which I was willing to accept something less than perfection.

But there were reasons for that. The first is that I knew that in Ivana I had a very special lady. I grew up with the American Dream of sharing life with a wife and children, and that's not something you just toss aside easily. I also stayed with Ivana because, as in most marriages, there was pressure to keep things intact.

We have three fantastic children to consider. I also dreaded the thought of disappointing my wonderful parents, Fred and Mary, who have stayed together for more than fifty years and who come from a generation that thinks of divorce as a basically selfish act—something that just doesn't happen.

There's nothing wrong, of course, with worrying about the effects of divorce on your children and the other people around you. The problem is that those considerations aren't enough to keep a marriage together. You can go for counseling, you can have heart-to-heart talks, you can stay together "for the sake of the kids." But in the end it's better for everyone if some couples part. Reconciliation is always possible, of course, but as I write, we seem to be headed in different directions.

This is by no means a snap judgment. I've discussed the situation with many people. I even thought, briefly, about approaching Ivana with the idea of an "open marriage." But I realized there was something hypocritical and tawdry about such an arrangement that neither of us could live with—especially Ivana. She's too much of a lady.

Ivana, I should point out for the sake of fairness, has never been as certain as I that we should part. She never really stopped loving me and I hope she never will. Likewise, I will always love Ivana. But that doesn't necessarily mean we should be together. Sometimes in a marriage only one person sees how far apart you've grown, and the other person for some reason can't see what's happened, or simply refuses to accept the idea. Though she was the first to go public with news of our breakup, Ivana was shocked about the separation, because on the surface everything was as it had been. Nothing about our day-to-day life or the way we got along had gotten worse or even changed noticeably. But it didn't matter that there was never a lot of yelling in our house, and no one was throwing vases or rolling pins around like in those old movies

—it was time to make the tough decisions and get on with the rest of our lives. Which was better for all concerned.

I think anyone who's finally seen some movement in his or her marital situation after years of deadlock will understand why I felt upbeat when the news was finally out. Ideally, of course, I would have liked to make the announcement myself, rather than having Ivana's public relations people leak the story when I was out of the country and couldn't give my side. But at least the long period of trying to make the best out of our situation was over. I would just get on with my life.

Looking back, I realize that I made a major miscalculation in underestimating how the press would play the news of my marital problems. I couldn't see Trump vs. Trump competing for very long with stories of Nelson Mandela's being released from prison after twenty-seven years, the reunification of Germany, and the demise of Drexel Burnham Lambert. But it was in the headlines for two solid months. I thought it was ridiculous—ridiculous and a little sick.

DON JUAN the front pages screamed, and that was followed by the infamous BEST SEX I EVER HAD story, in which an unnamed friend of a friend was quoted at length about what she supposedly heard someone say about me. According to the *Daily News* I gloated over the latter headline; according to the *National Enquirer*

I sobbed openly when I read it. Take your pick. Both accounts are as ridiculous as the story I was supposedly reacting to.

I usually read what's written about me, if only for laughs. But for a while there, I couldn't keep up with the torrent of Trump vs. Trump clips that were being generated each day by media all over the world. At one point, *Time*, *People*, and *Newsweek* all featured Trump stories on their covers, and Geraldo, Donahue, and others were busy interviewing every publicity-seeking lawyer, journalist, and therapist in town on the subject of Ivana and me. (Oprah has class and did not join in.) Even President Bush made a somewhat strained Trump divorce joke in a speech he gave during a visit to New York. This was like a bad dream.

For days several members of my staff were doing almost nothing but turning down interview requests, which were pouring in by the hundreds. The press was out of control. There was nothing I could do about it. Papers like the *Daily News* and the *New York Post* were selling an extra thirty thousand copies whenever they splashed the Trump story across their front pages. In view of the money they were making off Ivana's and my problems, they weren't about to let the story drop.

To keep a basically simple story alive for months, many writers and broadcasters had to switch, early on, from journalism to hysterical exaggeration. I'm sure that people like columnist Liz Smith simply sat down at the typewriter and tapped out whatever sounded good to them—or whatever Ivana's PR man, who is Ms. Smith's close friend, told them to write. In one paper I read that I was tearing up my prenuptial agreement, which provided for a settlement worth about $25 million, and instead was giving Ivana $100 million. That was utter nonsense, with numbers apparently snatched out of thin air. Other stories made me look like John, Robert, and Ted Kennedy combined. I've never had any trouble in bed, but if I'd had affairs with half the starlets and female athletes the newspapers linked me with, I'd have had no time to breathe.

A lot of people told me just to ignore the dumb and malicious reporting, but it ticked me off no end, especially as it began to extend to stories about the condition of my business empire. My track record had allowed me to secure millions of dollars' worth of financing simply by signing my name. If I'm perceived as a guy who is more interested in running around with women than in managing his business interests, that would make a difficult situation more complicated. The truth, meanwhile, was that I was as responsible as ever. I hadn't suddenly become obsessed with sex. I had simply separated from my wife because she and I had grown apart.

No other woman was responsible for the breakup. Marla Maples, the beautiful young actress who bore the brunt of the hysterical publicity, is a terrific person, but my relationship with her was not the cause of the trouble between Ivana and me. Marla was an easy target for the media because of her looks. Yet if I'd never met her, Ivana and I would still be separated.

Ivana and I were not the people we are now—we were kids, comparatively speaking—when we met at the Montreal Olympic games in 1976. She was a dazzling model in Canada then, having immigrated there from Czechoslovakia, where she'd made her mark as a competitive skier—an alternate, in fact, on that country's 1972 Olympic team. At the time I was really just getting started in the Manhattan real estate market, but I had a clear vision of what I wanted to—and eventually did—accomplish. I guess you could say we shared an interest in glamorous things. Beyond that, we were both young, ambitious, and not yet tied down to any real responsibilities.

I was especially carefree. I had a comfortable little studio apartment on Third Avenue in the city, and I maintained a life-style that was fairly commonplace then but that now, in an age when people are worried about dying from sex, is hard even to imagine. I didn't drink or take drugs; as far as stimulants go, I've yet to have my first cup of coffee. But I was out four or five nights a week, usually with a different woman each time, and I was enjoying myself immensely.

A lot of people expressed the thought, in the wake of the Trump vs. Trump blowup, that the nineties are a golden age of gossip and scandal. All I can say is they must not have been around, or don't remember, the Manhattan scene of fifteen years ago.

Wild things happened all the time back then, and nobody thought very much of it. For instance, one day a friend called me at the office and said he needed to set up a date for a certain well-known married woman. This woman was visiting from out of town and was, he said—using a typical swinging-seventies expression—"really hot."

I had a girlfriend at that time, and so did he, but I knew a guy named Ben who was very worldly-wise. Ben, I was sure, could serve as this woman's escort and be discreet about it. I called him immediately, and though he said he was tired and had been planning to stay home that night, Ben eventually agreed, as a personal favor to me, to take this woman out.

She turned out to be the wife of a man who was then the prime minister of a major country.

I'd heard stories about this lady, but I never thought much of them until that night. We met at the house of the friend who'd phoned me. After we'd all chatted for a while in the living room, the four of us who already knew each other drifted out to the kitchen, leaving Ben and Madame X in the living room to get better acquainted. Which they did. In fact, when we drifted back in, about ten minutes later, she and Ben were involved in an incredibly torrid scene on the couch.

I remember standing there and thinking to myself, "Well, Donald, you're not in Queens anymore."

At the time, believe it or not, that was just another night in the big city.

Ivana, in contrast to me, was already carrying around some heavy emotional baggage when we met. As we got to know each other better and started to fall in love, she told me about the marriage of convenience she'd had to undertake in order to get out of Czechoslovakia. Her real love at the time, she explained, was a young man who, tragically, had been killed in a car crash not long before she came to Canada. The loss was so painful that Ivana could hardly talk about it years later, and I didn't press her on it.

As far as I was concerned there was no need ever to bring it up again. The *New York Post* saw things differently. In a period when new journalistic lows were being hit every day, that paper outdid itself by rehashing those painful memories under the headline IVANA'S DARK PAST.

In fact, Ivana's real story was that of a woman who strove relentlessly to escape an Iron Curtain existence. She pushed hard at everything she did, kept her eyes open for every opportunity, and worked her way through Charles University in Prague.

I knew from the start that Ivana was different from

just about all of the other women I'd been spending time with. Good looks had been my top—and sometimes, to be honest, my only—priority in my man-about-town days. Ivana was gorgeous, but she was also ambitious and intelligent. When I introduced her to friends and associates, I said, "Believe me. This one's different." Everyone knew what I meant, and I think everyone sensed that I found the combination of beauty and brains almost unbelievable. I suppose I was a little naïve, and perhaps, like a lot of men, I had been taught by Hollywood that one woman couldn't have both. In any case, I saw this as a once-in-a-lifetime chance, and I didn't want it to slip through my fingers. Less than a year after Ivana and I met, we were married by the Reverend Norman Vincent Peale at Marble Collegiate Church in Manhattan.

It was a very exciting time in my life, but not so exciting that I rushed into marriage without a prenuptial agreement. Those documents weren't so common back then, but I had a belief that they were important for someone in my position.

A contract of this kind is a difficult subject to broach because there's no getting around the fact that planning for your breakup is not a very romantic way to spend an evening. One partner may even be insulted when his or her mate suggests having a prenuptial agreement drawn up. To a lot of people, it means you are giving up on a marriage before it even starts. They may be right about that. I've seen statistics that show that people who have prenuptial agreements are more likely to divorce than people who don't.

And yet, when all is said and done, I think a prenuptial agreement is a modern-day necessity.

When I first mentioned the need for one to Ivana, I kept my reasoning simple and honest—I tried to put myself in her place as we went along and discussed the various points.

The main thing I stressed was that I was building up a business that involved employees and creditors, and that because of the position I was in, I couldn't be faced with protracted litigation and uncertainty that would keep either of those groups from being paid. To do that would only damage my business, if not ruin it completely, and wind up hurting everyone involved. I also pointed out that it is much better for both sides to work out the details of a possible breakup while they are friends rather than after they have become enemies. From there I went on to say that some people who have prenuptial agreements get along better after marriage than those who don't and that they are certainly better off, if the marriage breaks up, than those who spend years fighting each other in the courts.

Those are very reasonable arguments—so reasonable that I would question the motives of a prospective mate who heard them and didn't agree to go along.

In any case, Ivana accepted the idea of a prenuptial agreement. We talked frankly about what we both wanted, and we didn't have any serious problems arriving at the specific terms of the agreement, either then or on the three later occasions when we made revisions—always in Ivana's favor—to reflect my increasing financial success.

In fact, we had no problems as a couple with anything, at least not for a while.

It's interesting how relationships, like children, go through different and fairly predictable stages. The first few years are usually so exciting that you're sure you're going to be one of those rare couples who go on forever. But then, no matter who you are, you get to the next stage, where the romantic haze clears, and you really see whether things are working out or not. Looking back, I see that Ivana and I haven't had much in common for quite a long time.

One of our problems was that we had directly opposing views of what it means, in terms of day-to-day life, to be wealthy and successful.

Ivana is what I'd call a traditionalist. She aspires to the aristocracy. She believes that people in our position should lead a certain kind of life—a life involving night after night of society people and gala society events, tuxedos and expensive ball gowns. She likes to travel in a world in which you summer here and weekend there and are always photographed with the right people. Down in Mar-a-Lago, our home in Palm Beach, she used to keep a fancy leather-bound book in which guests signed their names, and she would hand out printed schedules telling you when you'd play tennis, play golf, eat, and get a massage.

I understood, but have always hated that kind of life-style. In my opinion, the social scene—in New York, Palm Beach, or anywhere else, for that matter —is full of phonies and unattractive people who often have done nothing smarter than inherit somebody else's wealth—the Lucky Sperm Club, I call it. I'm a man with very simple tastes—not in building design, perhaps, but in most other things. I don't like rich sauces or fine wines. I like to eat steak rather than pheasant under glass. I prefer, on most nights, to sit in bed with the TV tuned to some movie or sports event and the phone not far away.

I'm not saying Ivana was totally wrong to want to be a big part of the social whirl. Many of those parties do raise a lot of money for charity and the arts, and to a certain extent, going to them and meeting the rare truly interesting or influential person can be good for business and intellectually stimulating. But you have only one life, and that's simply not how I wanted to live mine.

I remember complaining one evening to Abe Rosenthal, the brilliant former executive editor of *The New York Times* and now one of its columnists, about how much I hated going to dinner parties, especially when people insisted on "black tie" for a get-together they were having at their own house. "Isn't this the height of pretentiousness?" I asked. "Isn't it bad enough to have to go to these things and talk to these people without having to wear a tuxedo?"

"Ah, yes, Donald," Abe said. "But the ladies want it, and so we go along."

I just shook my head and said, "I guess you're right," because he was. But somehow my resentment deepened each time another awful evening rolled around.

What made the situation worse, I think, was that I spent most of my time running a big company and having control over what I did and whom I spent my time talking to. My nine-to-five day fascinated and energized me. But then, late in the afternoon, I'd often get a call from Ivana, reminding me of that night's engagement. "You'll be sitting next to Lord Some-body-or-Other at such-and-such an event," she'd say—and I'd suddenly feel like a low-level employee who'd just been handed some meaningless, mind-numbing assignment. Sometimes I'd get angry and say I wasn't going, and we'd fight about it on the phone. In the end, because I didn't want to disappoint or embarrass her, I'd almost always agree to go along. When I hung up the phone, though, I'd often say, loud enough, I suppose, for anyone standing in the hall outside my office to hear me, "My life is shit."

My entrance into the hotel-casino business also contributed to some of our problems because it pointed up a basic difference in our personalities.

I started to become deeply involved in the Atlantic

City scene in the early eighties, when I built the Trump Plaza and then acquired an almost-finished facility from Hilton that eventually became known as Trump Castle. Ivana became involved too. Partly because she needed something to do with her time, I asked her to oversee the Castle's operations. I can't say she didn't work hard at the job. Most mornings she'd fly down by helicopter, then fly back in time to have dinner with the kids and help them with their homework. She was always reading reports and attending meetings. Looking back, I realize Ivana did well, despite her lack of gaming-industry experience, or any natural affinity for the Atlantic City scene.

Actually, those two things go hand in hand. You don't have to *be* a gambler to be a success in the casino business; in fact, you're barred from gambling by law. What is absolutely necessary, however, is that you like and understand gamblers, from the slot-machine players, who are your bread and butter, to the high rollers, who can make a difference of millions of dollars in your bottom line in the course of one weekend. Frankly, the idea of risking hard-earned money on the toss of the dice or the spin of a wheel seems slightly ludicrous to me personally. But I do love the excitement of the scene, and I love hanging around with important casino customers. These are colorful, gutsy, unpretentious guys who usually come from modest backgrounds but who've managed to live by their wits and live rather lavishly.

They are, in other words, the exact opposite in many ways of the society people that Ivana liked to be associated with. And, in different ways, they are far more attractive, and certainly more real.

Fortunately, by 1988 I was in the process of buying the Plaza Hotel in New York, and that gave me the opportunity to ask Ivana to spend her days there instead of at the Castle, where she worked hard and did a good job. I knew that, as devoted as she was to the Castle, the chance to be in Manhattan and closer to the kids would prove irresistible.

Looking back, I see that bringing Ivana into the business was not as good an idea as I originally thought. The situation was my own fault, to a great degree. Ivana never really knew where she fit in; she had a somewhat ambiguous role in the organization—somewhere between the boss's wife (and representative) and an employee—and when lines are not drawn clearly, misunderstandings are inevitable. There were times when she'd make a decision and I'd overrule her, or I'd complain about some aspect of her operation and she'd get hurt and angry. "You want me to fail," she'd say.

Yet the tension and frustration I was feeling are only half the story. At the very time my marriage was going bad, I was starting to get attention from an unbelievable array of women.

Some of it was downright ridiculous. After I made an appearance on the Phil Donahue show to promote my first book, for example, I got mailbags full of flirtatious letters and outright propositions from women, many of whom included nude Polaroids of themselves in various poses. Somehow I didn't see myself going arm-in-arm in public with ladies of that ilk.

Yet it wasn't just gold diggers and would-be groupies who were showing interest in me. Some of the attention was coming from women who were quite interesting and even, in certain instances, great beauties—and often well known.

For all the trouble we had, though, and for all the opportunities that seemed to await me, moving out of the home I shared with Ivana and our three children in Trump Tower was the hardest personal decision I ever made. I wrestled with the idea for a long time.

Ultimately, I have to confess, the way I handled the situation was a cop-out. I never sat down calmly with Ivana to "talk it out," as I probably should have. Instead, I made careless comments, sometimes in public. The one that pushed her around the bend—and into Liz Smith's column—came in the *Playboy* interview that I did with the writer Glenn Plaskin. When Glenn asked me if my marriage was monogamous, I said, "I don't have to answer that." I went on to say, "I think any man enjoys flirtations, and if he said he didn't, he'd be lying or he'd be a politician trying to get the extra four votes. I think everybody likes knowing he's well responded to. Especially as you get into certain strata where there is an ego involved and a high level of success, it's important. People really like the idea that other people respond well to them.''

On one level, I was just speaking common sense. On another, I was, in effect, pushing the button that blew up our marriage. With that interview I virtually dared Ivana to go public with our problems—which she did, portraying herself as the woman scorned and easily winning the public's sympathy. Considering the example I'd set for her in what you might call image management, I would have been deeply disappointed in her if she had done anything else.

Ivana is a beautiful, strong, and shrewd woman who knows how to handle herself in almost any situation. She lives like a queen, and she's going to be all right no matter what happens. Fortunately for her, our nuptial agreement is ironclad and, if upheld in court, will make her financially secure for the rest of her life, provided she doesn't let expenses get completely out of hand.

I'm much more concerned—and less certain—about what the future holds for my children, Donny, Eric, and Ivanka. I know most fathers feel this way, but I think my kids are the greatest. Of course they have all the material advantages, and they always will.

Yet in many ways they had a difficult life even before they had to deal with their parents' separation and the media circus that accompanied it.

For security reasons, both their mother and I have to be extremely careful about being seen with them in public, and we never allow them to be photographed by the press. But it's a very hard situation to control, because we also want their lives to be as normal as possible. Not long ago a picture of Ivanka showed up in the *New York Post* in a story about her dancing school. "The Littlest Trump Prepares for a Performance," the caption said. Any other little girl, and her parents, would have been thrilled to be singled out for such special attention. But I was angry when I saw that photo and I complained.

I *have* to protect my kids that way, and yet, by growing up wealthy and in a cocoon, they are, I know, actually at a disadvantage in developing the skills they'll need to succeed on a grand scale. My kids are fine, and if you have energy, confidence, and intelligence, you've got an unbeatable combination. Unfortunately, if you look at the record you'll see that the children of successful people usually lack one or more of those qualities. Many of them, sad to say, are utter fools and failures. You never know for certain until they're actually put to the test. Maybe I'm just being an overprotective father, but if I have any influence in the matter, my kids may well be managers, not entrepreneurs. It would give me a great kick to know they were just living a good life and maintaining the Trump empire—whatever that turns out to be when this weird adventure of mine is all over.

This chapter has been the most difficult for me to deal with for many reasons. I'm not comfortable discussing my feelings, and the truth is that I don't know what the outcome of my separation from Ivana will be. I've joked about ending sections of this book with a question mark, and this is certainly one of them.

FOUR

LIFE AT THE TOP

ONE of the most popular chapters in *The Art of the Deal* described a week in my life. I said then that there is no such thing as a typical period for me.

However, as I step back and look at my life, I do see certain trends emerging. During the last few years, for example, I've done a lot of battling. I've fought hard to get certain assets. I've fought to get contractors to live up to their obligations. And I've probably fought hardest of all to preserve a reputation that has often been under serious assault.

I can't win them all, but I win more of those battles than I lose. And I'm still learning something—about business, about people, about life—from each encounter.

While working on this book, I've been jotting down thoughts and recording certain events almost as soon as they occurred. Here, to give you a sample of what it's like, are some recent scenes.

9:00 A.M. My father, Fred, calls from his office in Brooklyn just to touch base and chat. We talk on the phone probably a dozen times a week.

My father and I have a great relationship. I call him Daddy-O or Pops, and he is equally affectionate with me in his sometimes gruff way. I think that after some initial skepticism about my high-profile deals and my branching out beyond real estate, my father has come to enjoy my success.

Which is not to say that he's lost any of his tough exterior. This is a man who never lets you forget that he's your father. "Ah, what do you know about this business or that?" he'll sometimes ask me, still. He thinks only in terms of success. It's never spoken, but you get the message if you're his son.

A lot of people have said that I push myself so hard because I am in competition with my father. That's really not true, although I suspect every son, to some degree, wants to outdo his father. If something about Dad does spur me on, it's the tremendous confidence he's shown in me. I'm always trying to justify that.

12:00 noon One of my executives in Atlantic City calls to tell me that a certain Arab sheik dropped $900,000 at the Trump Castle over the weekend. On the face of it, that's not so unusual—a lot of high rollers routinely win or lose amounts like that at the baccarat or blackjack tables—but this guy played nothing but slot machines. You have to work hard to lose that much at the slots in one weekend. In fact, it took this particular customer four solid days of shoving one-hundred-dollar tokens into side-by-side machines.

Gamblers are truly a breed apart.

2:00 P.M. A guy I'm just getting to know and am thinking of doing a deal with calls and asks if I want to play a round of golf with him the following afternoon. My first reaction is to say no, I'm too busy to be away from the office. But then I think about it a little more and decide to go.

Playing golf with a business associate, in my experience, is seldom a waste of time. That's because golf is a game that quickly reveals a lot about a person's character and priorities. I find it interesting to watch the ways various kinds of people use the handicap system, which in theory allows people of different abilities to compete against one another on an equal basis.

I have one friend, for example, who insists that he's a nine handicap. Some of the people I play with joke that we can make a living playing this guy at nine when he really should be a seventeen or an eighteen. He absolutely never wins, but he doesn't care; he'd rather go around bragging about what a low handicap he has.

Then there is the other kind of golfer—the guy who should be a four, five, or six handicap but who plays to a thirteen, fourteen, or fifteen. This, of course, makes him virtually impossible to beat.

As for myself, I've been playing since I was about eighteen years old, and at one point I got my handicap down to a three at tough courses. So you could say that I'm not a bad golfer. My personality is such, though, that I would much rather win at a high handicap than lose at a low one.

5:30 P.M. I call a man I know who runs a public company that's not doing so well. When his secretary tells me that she'll give him the message when he gets back from vacation, I'm more than a little surprised.

"Really? That's what you told me when I called the first time—about a week and a half ago," I say.

"Yes, I know, Mr. Trump," she replies, "but he's been away the whole time, and he hasn't called in yet."

Hearing that, I immediately realize that this man, despite having some potential, will never make it in business, and his company will suffer as long as he's in control. Executives who leave the office and don't call in at least daily are always in for some unpleasant surprises. And so are that company's stockholders.

When I'm out of the office, I call in ten or so times a day—from my car, from pay phones, even from the golf course. That's probably excessive, but I'd rather err on the side of making too much contact. In any business, there are always fires springing up, and the faster you can put them out, the better.

———

9:00 A.M. I get a call from Robert Morgenthau, the brilliant Manhattan district attorney, who tells me that I have been selected to be the honoree at the seventy-fifth annual Police Athletic League dinner, a gala affair that will be held in the grand ballroom of the Plaza Hotel. I know that PAL, which helps underprivileged youngsters throughout the city, means a lot to Bob, and so I ask him if there's anything I can do to ensure that the evening will be a success.

"Well, actually," Bob says, "I was wondering who you thought would make a good chairman."

It's a good question. I know from my experience with these big charity affairs that picking the chairman is crucial. The person you want for that job, ideally, is someone who not only sells tickets but also brings in people who write big checks. As it happens, I know perhaps the ultimate guy for the job: Henry Kravis of Kohlberg Kravis Roberts.

Henry, the mastermind behind the $24 billion leveraged buyout of RJR Nabisco, is one of the great dealmakers of this century. He and I are friends more than business rivals. Still, we're both competitive guys with healthy egos, and I have to admit I am getting a charge out of the idea of Henry selling tickets to a dinner honoring me.

But then I think of a way to have even a little more fun with the situation.

"Bob," I say to District Attorney Morgenthau, "I know you don't know Henry. But I really think it would be better if you called him yourself and asked him to serve as chairman." Bob laughs when I say that because he knows exactly what I am up to.

A certain source at KKR later told me what happened.

When it was announced that District Attorney Robert Morgenthau was on the phone, a hush fell over Henry's office. Henry is a totally honest guy, but you have to realize that he knows Bob only as a brilliant prosecutor who is indicting various people and companies almost on a daily basis.

As he picked up the phone, Henry was already breaking into a sweat. "Yes, sir, Mr. Morgenthau, is there anything I can do for you?" he asked.

"Well, yes, there is, Mr. Kravis," said Bob, who then paused a minute to heighten the effect of the call. "In two months we'll be honoring Donald Trump at the PAL dinner, and he asked if you'd be his chairman.''

Bob later told me that never before has a chairmanship of a charity dinner been accepted with such enthusiasm and gusto. "Oh, yes, certainly," Henry said. "Serve as chairman? I couldn't think of anything I'd rather do."

With Henry as chairman, the dinner was a great success.

10:30 A.M. Debbie Allen, the dancer and singer, calls from her beauty parlor to say how much she enjoyed serving as a judge for the Miss America Pageant in Atlantic City. I agree that it was great fun, especially since I was able to arrange things so that for the first time the celebrity judges didn't have to spend an entire week watching all the preliminary contests. Instead, those of us who did the judging were able to come in on the night of the finals, review the competition, and then be on our way. The result was that the pageant was not limited in its choice of judges to the kinds of celebrities who can spend weeks hanging around and not doing very much in the middle of the summer.

12:00 noon One of my in-house attorneys comes in to tell me that Stanley Friedman has been sentenced to twelve years in prison. Friedman, a former Bronx county chairman, was once among the most powerful politicians in New York—until he was indicted for taking kickbacks from a company trying to sell computer equipment to the city's Parking Violations Bureau.

Friedman, who was told to take his trial out of the city and up to white-lace Connecticut, got some terrible legal advice. I sincerely believe, after talking to lawyers and reporters who covered the various Koch administration scandals, that in a New York courtroom Friedman would have come off as just another hard-driving politician and would have beaten the rap. But in Connecticut he was viewed as a wise guy—a tough, ethnic city slicker who was too cute for his own good and needed to be punished.

Of course, it's Stanley and not his lawyers who will pay, and pay dearly, for the mistake of moving the case out of the city. Stanley Friedman got a stiffer sentence than many child molesters and murderers—and many people at the time felt he should not even have been convicted.

2:00 P.M.   I get a call from a friend who works on a magazine that has recently been taken over by a larger publishing company. I ask him how things are going, and he says, "Donald, it's a disaster. This used to be a great publication, but now it's only a matter of time before we're all out looking for other jobs."

What happened was this: The new company asked the old owner to stay on and run things, but the guy who started it all suddenly seemed to lose his old drive and zest. He doesn't come in until about ten in the morning; then he putters around a bit, takes a two-hour lunch, and goes home at five.

I'm not surprised to hear this story. In theory, having the former owner stay on and provide stability and expertise sounds fine. But in reality it almost never works. What you wind up with is a so-called leader who is more interested in buying a new home, managing his investments, and planning a vacation than in pushing hard to make sure the company is a success.

3:30 P.M. A few days after I appeared on the Phil Donahue show, Norma brings me a handwritten letter from Barbara Bush. "Dear Donald," it says. "Just a note—As I was leaving the house this morning I heard you being attacked by Phil Donahue. You were wonderful! Barbara." Mrs. Bush is a classy lady.

8:00 P.M. I head off to the CNN studios to do an interview on the televised *Larry King Live* show. I love doing Larry's show. One of the things that make him a great interviewer is that, unlike Dick Cavett and a host of other lesser talents, Larry is able to let his guests have center stage when the lights are on and the tape is rolling.

One of Larry's first questions this evening is an especially perceptive one. "You always seem to catch people off guard and then go for the jugular,'' Larry observes. ''How do you do it?''

Instead of answering directly, I look at him, assume an expression of mild disgust, and say, ''Larry, you have bad breath. Really bad breath.'' I then back away from him.

Larry is honestly startled. He looks around, he starts to say something, he shuffles his papers. He really doesn't know what to do. And then, a second or two later, he figures out what I am up to—namely, demonstrating how to throw an adversary totally off stride with an unexpected comment.

Larry loved my little maneuver once he figured it out. I'm sure he sensed that, in a perverse way, our awkward exchange made for good TV and had nothing to do with his breath.

9:00 A.M. The manager of one of my buildings calls to say that Larry Hagman, the star of the TV series *Dallas*, doesn't like the replacement tiles that were used in the bathroom of his apartment after we had to do some repair work. Should we rip them out and give him others?

This may not sound like something that requires an executive decision. On the other hand, I've learned a lot about building materials over the years, and I actually enjoy working with bricks, tile, carpet, and wallpaper.

"Okay, let's take out the off-white and give him the tan," I tell the building manager. "I think what Mr. Hagman wants is a richer, warmer look."

I guess I was right about that because after we made the switch I heard no further complaints. A waste of time? Actually, I considered it thirty seconds well spent.

11:00 A.M. I head out to La Guardia Airport, where my plane is waiting to take me to Palm Beach. When I arrive at the plane, though, there's a stranger at the door waiting to greet me.

"Who are you?" I ask.

"I'm your new pilot," this guy says. "Your management company hired me."

Right away I don't like the situation. It's true that I did retain a management company to take care of the plane. But I had an agreement with them that I would have the power of hiring and firing any pilot. The reason is simple: I'm not a great flier, and I feel much better knowing I have personally selected the person who will have my life in his hands.

"I think what I'm going to do," I tell this new pilot, "is take a pass on this flight. First of all, I don't know who you are. And second, I don't have tremendous respect for a management company that would do something like this."

I then ask my driver to take me over to the main terminal, where I catch a commercial flight. I'll be calling my management company, I know, as soon as I get back.

8:30 A.M.   I sit down with Dennis Connor, the skipper who won two America's Cups for the United States, to discuss a plan he has for gaining some publicity for my Atlantic City hotels. Dennis is the world's greatest sailor, a true champion and a very savvy guy. But this particular idea of his, which involves a series of yacht races, sounds very expensive and extremely complicated. Besides, no benefits will be reaped from the plan, as I understand it, until around 1993. The way my internal clock works, that's much too far down the road to even contemplate.

I listen awhile and then start to turn the conversation around. I am starting to think about building a new and much bigger yacht, I tell Dennis. If I do go ahead, and maybe even if I don't, I'll be looking to sell the *Trump Princess*. It occurs to me that because of the circles he travels in, Dennis might know of a buyer.

Dennis is thrown for a moment by my suggestion, but then he says yes, he does in fact know some people who might be potential buyers for my boat. As far as I'm concerned, I tell him, we have an arrangement that will give him a handsome commission if I do decide to sell and he brokers the deal.

When our meeting breaks up a few minutes later, he's happy because he's got a potentially lucrative opportunity. And I'm happy because I've just retained a very impressive salesman who will cost me nothing unless he does me a big service. The funny thing is, neither of us envisioned these possibilities when he walked in the door five minutes ago.

10:30 A.M. Before I get around to calling them, someone from the management company that I'd hired to take care of my airplane calls me and asks what the problem is with the new pilot.

"First, tell me what happened to the old pilot," I say.

"We had to let him go," this guy says. "He was demanding two thousand dollars more a year."

When I hear this, I almost go crazy. I'd interviewed that pilot myself, and I was very impressed with him. He'd been in the Air Force and flown in Vietnam. Besides, his performance was impeccable. When he landed the plane, you couldn't even feel it touch down.

"You've got to be kidding," I say to the management company representative. "You know, for two thousand dollars a year you lost a very good man."

Not to mention, I could have added, a very good client.

The next call I place is to my original pilot.

We talk for a while about what had happened with my management company, and during the course of the conversation I mention that I am paying two dollars a gallon for fuel. "Gee, Mr. Trump," he says, "I can get the same fuel for fifty-five cents a gallon."

I don't know, off the top of my head, how many gallons of airplane fuel I use each year, but whatever it is, that sounds like a significant savings.

"Listen, I have an idea," I say to him. "How would you like to come back to work for me as a kind of pilot-manager? You'll handle everything about the plane—budgets, supplies, and the rest of the crew— in addition to flying me around."

He agrees on the spot, and I call back the management company and say I no longer require their services.

It was a move that over the course of the next year saved me more than $400,000. In a subsequent lawsuit against the company I won another $400,000 as compensation for their mismanagement.

3:00 P.M.   I come out of a meeting and head back to my office in Trump Tower, walking three blocks along Fifth Avenue. It is a break in the day that gives me time to sort out my thoughts.

At one time I'd been thinking about calling this book *Everybody Hates a Winner*. To me, that title rang true because, frankly, I sense a lot of jealousy and hostility from many people I do business with or see socially. Some of the most successful people, I've noticed, can associate only with people less successful than themselves. When they're around someone who gets more attention than they do and has accomplished more than they have, they display a major personality complex, acting nervous and uneasy—and I'm sure they say vicious things behind the more successful person's back.

But my short trip through the streets makes me realize something else about people. As I walk along, about twenty-five perfect strangers wave and shout, "Hi, Donald," and "How're you doing, Donald," and "Keep up the good work." One thing this proves to me is that the average working man or woman is a lot better adjusted and more secure than the supposedly successful people who stare down at them from the penthouses.

I guess the truth is that not everybody hates a winner.

6:00 P.M. A guy I barely know, some New York society fool, calls. "Ho, ho, ho," he says, with a kind of forced laughter. "I've been reading the *Doonesbury* cartoons about you. You've got to admit they're hilarious."

"Oh, do I have to admit that?" I ask. "I might admit they were funny if they made any sense. I went to school, I always got good marks, but I just don't get these so-called jokes. If you understand what this guy is driving at, please explain it to me."

"Oh, but Donald . . ." he says.

"No, really, please explain it to me," I say.

Of course, he can't.

The *Doonesbury* strip is a lesson in pure salesmanship. Garry Trudeau, the guy who draws it, has a lot of people convinced that he's hip and irreverent and that his comic strip is the thing to read. He's such a good salesman that it doesn't matter that he lacks the talent to back up his claims. I was in total agreement when I saw an article in *Rolling Stone* in which George Carlin, a guy who *is* really hip and irreverent, called the *Doonesbury* cartoon extremely overrated and said that he just didn't get what everyone thought was so funny.

Neither do I, George, although if Garry Trudeau wants to keep immortalizing me in print, perhaps I have to consider it an honor. Trudeau's wife, Jane Pauley, is much more talented than he is.

———

9:00 A.M. I get a nice letter from Helen Gurley Brown asking if I'd pose for a centerfold in *Cosmopolitan* magazine. I laugh and show the note to Blanche Sprague, my executive vice president in charge of sales, who happens to have dropped by the office. "Maybe I should do it," I say, half kiddingly. "Besides," I say, "it is kind of an honor."

Blanche looks at me like I'm crazy. This is a woman who doesn't mince words. I often tell her she's the ultimate New York mouth. "This is your idea of an *honor*?" she asks.

Just to tease her, I put the letter aside as if I'm still

thinking about it. But the next day I ask Norma to draft a response saying that unfortunately I'm unable to take advantage of the opportunity.

11:30 A.M.　I get together with a team of architects to talk about the restoration of the ballroom at the Plaza Hotel. I want to go first class, I tell them—regild the moldings with real gold and generally re-create the lavish look the Plaza had when it opened in 1907. They listen, nod, and then tell me that their fee is 4 percent of the cost of the restoration.

To me, that sounds like a ridiculous way to do business. "Wait a minute," I say. "Suppose you recommend I use onyx instead of tile on the floor. Onyx is twenty times more expensive. Why should I pay you thousands of dollars just for saying 'onyx' instead of 'tile.' That doesn't make sense to me."

"But, Mr. Trump," they stammer. "That's the way it works."

"Excuse me," I say, "but I don't think so."

In the end, I hired those architects for the Plaza, but they worked for a flat fee.

2:00 P.M.　A friend calls and starts singing the praises of his personal trainer. I should hire this guy to come over every morning, he says, and put me through a strenuous workout.

I tell him no thanks. I find exercise boring. I don't

have the patience for it. I depend on golf, a little tennis, and whatever walking I do to keep me fit. And I guess it works, to a degree, at least. I know that sometimes, on the spur of the moment, if I'm going up to my apartment in Trump Tower to see my kids or for some other reason, I'll walk up all sixty-eight floors. I can still do it without breathing too hard.

4:00 P.M. I've got a deal cooking, and the calls are coming hot and heavy now. It strikes me, as I'm moving from line to line, that it probably wouldn't be physically possible to take or make more calls than I do at certain points in the day.

I believe there is an art to handling telephone traffic. The first thing you need to remember is to keep the conversation short. Not only will you make your points more strongly, but if you limit your calls to thirty seconds or less, as I try to do, you'll be able to start and finish one phone conversation while your secretary is initiating another.

Another thing that saves time is to place your just-keeping-in-touch calls during the lunchtime hours, when you're virtually certain the people you're phoning won't be around. What I do—especially with people I want to pay my respects to but don't really need to have a conversation with—is to leave messages saying Donald Trump called to say hello but there's no need to call him back. That way, in about ten seconds, I can accomplish almost the same thing I would by shooting the breeze with someone for five or ten minutes.

The real key, though, is having a good secretary. You have to have someone with split-second timing who can sense when your conversation is winding down, how important various people are, and how many levels of receptionists and secretaries surround each person on your call list. Although I don't use one myself, I believe it can help to have a buzzer so you can signal whoever is placing your phone calls to start dialing the next one.

I know this may sound silly. And I'm not saying this is the ultimate way to live. But if you inhabit the world of dealmaking, it sure as hell helps to be able to make the maximum number of calls at crucial moments.

9:30 A.M. I get a call from Guido Civetta, a contractor I'd hired to put in the foundation for Trump Palace, a fifty-six-story condominium I'm building on Sixty-ninth Street and Third Avenue. Usually, when someone like this phones, it's about a problem or a delay, so I brace myself and get ready to scream. But a minute later I'm shocked to hear Guido telling me that the foundations are in and finished two months ahead of schedule.

This is, of course, great news. Not only will his speed save me many times the cost of his contract, but it will allow me to have the building I wanted. One reason I was rushing to get the foundations completed was that the city was seriously considering changing the zoning on the East Side of Manhattan. If they had, I would have been forced to scale down the size of my building considerably. But because the foundations are in, I am automatically vested in the old and more generous zoning limits.

Guido is justifiably proud of what he's accomplished. I thank him sincerely, and then, just as we are about to hang up, I say, "By the way, what kind of car does your wife drive?"

"A Cadillac," Guido says, "but I've got to get her a new one soon because hers is starting to get a bit old."

"Don't bother, Guido," I tell him. "Just tell me what color you want, and it will be over at your house this afternoon."

11:30 A.M. I attend a press conference for the Tour de Trump, a bicycle race I sponsor. While I'm sitting on the dais, a reporter asks Greg LeMond—the great American cyclist and a two-time winner of the Tour de France—if he considers his competitors to be his friends. "Oh, sure I do," Greg replies cheerfully.

Hearing that, I realize that bicycle racing must be very different from business. I can't imagine any circumstances in which I would consider one of my competitors to be a friend.

7:30 P.M. I go to dinner with a few close friends at Le Cirque, one of New York's hottest and most exclusive restaurants. The room is filled with very successful people from a variety of fields, all of whom are acting quite blasé about being in one another's presence—New York is a town not easily impressed with anybody. Then Richard Nixon enters, accompanied by his old friend Bebe Rebozo. A hush falls over the restaurant, and heads turn to look.

For a few long moments it seems as if nothing happens, and no one moves. The reaction, it seems to me, is a silent tribute to toughness.

The incident reminds me of a time not long ago when I'd ridden back with the former president in my plane from a charity event in Texas. Barbara Walters, a good friend of mine, also came along for the ride.

As we flew back to New York, Nixon spent several hours telling fascinating stories about world events and politics. Early on in the trip, Barbara got excited by the prospect of somehow capturing this side of Richard Nixon—relaxed and speaking off-the-cuff—for her *20/20* show or perhaps one of her specials.

"Mr. President," she asked, "why don't you come on ABC and let me interview you? This is extremely interesting stuff."

Nixon, though, acted as if he had some kind of hearing problem and refused to answer or even to acknowledge the question.

This naturally resulted in Barbara's asking again, "Mr.

President, we would love to do something on you.''

But again Nixon just kept talking, as if she'd never said anything. ''When I was in China . . . ,'' he'd say, starting another story every time she asked about an interview.

Barbara and I were both mystified by his reaction, or lack of one, and after four or five attempts she finally gave up and stopped asking. It was only later that she learned that Nixon considered ABC to be one of his worst attackers over the years, and that he was especially put off by the fact that Barbara's network was then planning to broadcast the miniseries *The Final Days*, a not-very-flattering look at the end of his presidency.

Once I knew that, I realized that he had handled the matter in true Nixonian fashion. Rather than hemming and hawing, or even saying no, he had gone a step further and had refused even to acknowledge the request.

I've seen some real killers in my line of work, but Richard Nixon makes them look like babies. The man is a rock, like him or not, and when you think of how far he's come back and the things he's endured, he's even more amazing.

10:00 A.M.   A major fashion show is going on at the Plaza, but I've just gotten word from one of my people that a prominent designer has decided to preview his new line of clothes someplace else. He is the only designer who has broken away and moved his show outside the Plaza, and that, frankly, annoys me a bit —especially since he didn't hesitate to call me once in a true emergency situation.

I'm referring to an incident that happened a couple of years earlier. Very late one night the phone rang in my bedroom in New York and it was the designer, whom I then regarded as a friend. This was shortly before he entered a program for substance abuse. It was a very weird conversation.

"Hang on," I said. Then I had some of my people rush over and take the designer to the nearest hospital. A few hours later I called there to see how he was doing, and a nurse said, "If you hadn't gotten the patient to the hospital so soon, it would have been too late."

The designer never acknowledged that I helped him out that night. I've learned that some people have a strange definition of gratitude.

10:30 A.M.   I get a call from Dick Wilhelm, the vice president and general manager of the Plaza. Kitty Dukakis, he says, has checked into the hotel. Could I call her suite to welcome her?

I'm sure Mrs. Dukakis is a lovely and brave woman, and I know that the personal touch is important in the hotel business. But making small talk and being an official greeter are two of the things I like to do least.

I put off making the call for a couple of hours hoping

the obligation will just go away. When I finally do reach her, Mrs. Dukakis turns out to be a gracious lady who has some questions about the Plaza restoration. What I've been putting off turns out to be an easy couple of minutes after all.

11:00 A.M. A representative for Sarah, the Duchess of York, calls and asks if Sarah can borrow my helicopter on her next trip to New York. I'm not really surprised. My helicopter was built in France, to the highest military standards. It has a reputation for being one of the safest and smoothest-riding helicopters around. I only wish my friends Steve, Mark, and Jon had taken it instead of the chartered Agusta that brought them to their deaths.

I tell the man on the phone that I'd be honored if the duchess would use my helicopter.

12:00 noon I read in the paper about a young woman who has been raped, beaten, and thrown off the roof of a tenement in Brooklyn. That she has survived is something of a miracle. The incident gets less publicity than the infamous Central Park jogger case, but in a way it is remarkably similar, except for one detail. The victim in this case is a poor black woman who, judging from the news accounts, faces huge medical bills and probably isn't, at the present time anyway, in a position to pay them.

Perhaps because I'm still enraged about the Central

Park case, this drives me wild. The first thing I do is arrange to pay the woman's expenses until she is back on her feet. I contribute a substantial amount of money each year to various charities, and I feel a need to help this particular woman.

The next thing I decide is to take a ride out to Kings County Hospital, where the woman is receiving treatment. I want to meet her, tell her how brave I think she is, and also focus attention on the fact that crime is not a racial issue. I'm well aware that inner-city people are victimized by crime much more than others.

As it turned out, my plan worked—at least, the press showed up, and I think we made our point. I *know* I impressed my driver, who was getting more and more lost until I realized what was happening and gave him a few quick directions that brought us straight to the hospital. I spent a lot of time in Brooklyn growing up, and I know the streets.

11:45 P.M. I'm sitting and watching a guy on *The Tonight Show*. He is an actor whom I've greatly admired for years for his cool tough-guy roles. But now there he is, sitting in front of millions of people, telling an all-too-familiar story of depression, drugs, and booze. After he reached the heights, he says, he spent several years in a kind of fog, feeling guilty about his success and trying to destroy himself and everything he'd worked for.

Perhaps he got something out of baring his soul like that on national TV. It's certainly become fashionable for famous people to flaunt their weaknesses. My reaction, though, is to switch quickly to the Ted Turner channel that shows nothing but old movies, made in the days when Hollywood knew how to provide the public with heroes and glamour.

10:00 A.M. It's time for the weekly meeting on the Trump City project that I'm planning for the West Side railroad yards. But as usual, I won't be there.

While a lot of work is still being done on the project, I had put Trump City on the back burner for the time being, at least in my own mind. The reason is simple: I want this to be a spectacular project, perhaps even my crowning achievement as a real estate developer. What I don't want it to be is a series of compromises and concessions that won't do the job of competing successfully with the development of the New Jersey waterfront, a development that is sucking the lifeblood out of New York City.

In the meantime, the meetings go on. Anthony Gliedman—a former New York City commissioner whom I hired away from Ed Koch—will be there, in the conference room just down the hall from my office. As usual, they'll discuss what's happening with the seventy-eight-acre site, which I intend to develop into a residential and office complex, including the world's tallest building.

If I'm going to get what I want in terms of zoning and approvals, I know I have to be patient, wait for the pendulum to swing and for times to get tough again, as they were in the mid-seventies. If you look around at New York and the nation's other major cities, you'll see that that's already starting to happen. So I'll just bide my time until the city decides it really needs the taxes, the housing, and the billions of dollars in revenue from shopping that Trump City will bring—and then I'll begin pushing the project toward reality.

As for the community groups that oppose the project, they claim to be fighting to preserve their neighborhood, but in truth most of them like to fight for the sake of fighting. If I were building a huge nature preserve on the site, they'd be passing around a petition. What it comes down to is that those people are selfish; they don't want to share what they have with anybody else. They say the West Side can't handle more people. That's nonsense. The fact is, there were more people living in that area in the forties than there are today. The other thing they fail to realize is that Trump City is going to be an architectural masterpiece, one of the most exciting things that've happened to New York in several decades.

The way I look at it is I have truth and beauty on my side. So all I have to do is be patient and I will win.

6:30 P.M. Watching the news, I see dramatic footage of Hurricane Hugo wreaking havoc in Puerto Rico. I get a call from Andrew Stein, the New York City Council president, and he tells me that he has a plan to help.

"Donald," he says, "why don't you and I make some phone calls to see if we can get some of our friends to donate food and other emergency supplies to the relief effort down there. Also, could you loan us a Trump Shuttle plane to fly it all down there whenever they are ready?"

I like the idea, and a few days later Andy and his wife, Lynn, and Bronx councilman José Rivera are flying to Puerto Rico with bottled water, electrical generators, clothes, and other vital items.

8:30 A.M. I go out to visit a 298-unit senior citizens complex I own in East Orange, New Jersey. I built the Pavillion, as it's called, with my father not long after I graduated from Wharton in 1968, and to be perfectly honest, it makes zero economic sense to me. But I don't think I'll ever sell the complex. I like the people there, and I like that I'm running it better than anybody else would. I don't think of it any differently than I do any of my other properties. I run it as if it were a superluxury building, and the senior citizens there seem to appreciate that.

11:00 A.M. A photographer from a magazine comes to the office to take a picture of me with three of my female executive vice presidents—Barbara Res, Blanche Sprague, and Susan Heilbron—for the magazine's cover. I'm in the middle of about six deals, so I'm not exactly pleased with the interruption. But looking back, I'm glad I took the time to pose. Owen Edwards, the writer assigned to do an article about the women in my organization, got it right. "Donald Trump . . . has consistently put his money on women," Edwards wrote, "betting on them to succeed in situations where failure would be costly. And he has done it far more than the many businessmen who talk a good game but keep their inner circles as masculine as a Masai lion hunt."

I'm not a crusader for feminism, and I'm not against it, either. I'm just oblivious to a person's gender when it comes to hiring people and handing out assignments.

2:00 P.M. I head out to California for a press conference to announce that I've acquired the Ambassador Hotel site in Los Angeles. This is my first project on the West Coast, and it's not going to be an easy one. The Ambassador itself is a run-down mess that had closed a year earlier, after a long period of decline. I want to raze the structure and replace it with a dazzling billion-dollar commercial and residential complex that would be a kind of Trump City West.

I already know there's going to be resistance, if

only because the hotel was the scene of a historic event: Robert Kennedy's assassination. To me, though, that's not a good enough reason for residents of the city to keep living with a structure that is unsafe, antiquated, and a blight on the landscape. As I say in the announcement I prepared, I want to replace the Ambassador with "buildings of architectural distinction and true California style." It's going to be a long battle to get the right zoning and approvals. But then, as I've said elsewhere, the battles are often the best part of life.

————————————

8:00 A.M.   I'm driving up Third Avenue when I decide to swing by the construction site of the Trump Palace. This is probably the best neighborhood in the world for single people, I'm thinking—but then I look up at the building from a block away, and I see something I don't like. The one concrete terrace that has been poured looks wrong to me. Not very wrong, but enough to make me reach for my car phone and call Blanche Sprague and Andy Weiss, who are overseeing the construction.

Blanche's first reaction is that I'm crazy. She has just come back from the site, she says, and everything is fine.

"Call the architect," I say. "I'm sure he'll see what I mean." She does and then calls me back quickly to say that he agrees with her.

"Well, then," I say, "why don't you both go back to the site and check it out with the construction supervisor."

A couple of hours later, Blanche calls back. The pitch of that terrace was off by just a couple of inches, she says, but it *was* off. The crew is going to repair the first one, and make sure that the rest are done according to specifications.

I've got good eyesight, but more important, I know how to build. That's my strong point and probably what I'll always be best at. I've thought about getting into the movie business, publishing, and TV. I still may do any or all of those things. But to me, there's nothing more exciting or satisfying than putting up a building.

2:00 P.M. I arrive in Atlantic City for a press conference announcing that the Rolling Stones will be performing a series of concerts at Trump Plaza—and promptly have my illusions about that rock group shattered. I've always been a fan of their music and in the future I may still be. But to put it mildly, the Stones impress me this day as a bunch of major jerks.

Their basic problem is that they are not the sole stars of the show, as they have been most of their "adult" lives. The press is going wild with the Trump vs. Trump story at this point, and as soon as I step into the room, I start getting a lot of questions about my recent separation from Ivana. When the Stones realize what is happening, they send word that they refuse to come onstage to discuss their concerts. "All this commotion is distracting to Mick and the boys," one of their people says.

Rather than cause a scene, I decide to step aside and let the Stones have the stage to themselves, if that is so important to them. On the way out, however, I pass them in a hallway, and they are a sorry sight. I have never seen them at such close range, and now I notice that years of hard living show on their faces, which look pale and haggard far beyond their age. (It's no wonder, I think, that they wear heavy makeup and insist that their lighting be just so.) Surrounding them on all sides are their bodyguards—a surprisingly puny, mean-spirited bunch of wise guys who shove and rough up people who aren't even in their way. As I brush past, Mick Jagger calls out my name, sticks out his hand, and flashes a phony smile. I just keep walking.

10:00 P.M. I am at a dinner party at Adnan Khashoggi's New York City apartment when I overhear him talking to a beautiful female.

"You should become a Moslem," he says flirtatiously. "Then I could make you one of my wives."

"I don't think I'd like that kind of arrangement," the woman says, laughing.

"Ah, but you don't understand," he says. "Where there are many wives, there must be much love."

She laughs again and changes the subject. It occurs to me that Khashoggi is irrepressible. At the time this is happening his fortunes have diminished greatly, and he is awaiting trial on corruption charges in connection with his relationship to Ferdinand and Imelda Marcos. Through it all, though, he remains the same cool character, smiling, having dinner parties, and talking to beautiful women. Amazing. (He ultimately beat the rap with total grace and style.)

9:00 A.M. At a time when news about my financial difficulties is making daily headlines and I'm locked in negotiations with bankers, I begin to get letters from people offering their support. Some of the notes contain checks for five or ten dollars. I return the money, of course, with a note of my own. But I find the gesture truly touching.

Most of the phone calls I'm getting are nice, too, but I can't help noticing that some people call more for their benefit than mine. They are trying to make themselves feel they've done their good deed for the day, I guess. But every time I find myself in a conversation like that, I just roll my eyes and think, Here we go again.

11:00 A.M. I visit the Winged Foot Country Club in Westchester County, New York. I love golf, and when I first joined Winged Foot, in the mid-seventies, I was there often and got to know some of the members quite well. As I got busier and busier, though, I found it increasingly difficult to get up to the club. This is my first visit in perhaps eight or ten years.

Winged Foot itself seems virtually unchanged, with its lush green lawns and handsome clubhouse, and seeing it brings a lot of good memories. "How's Ben Allen?" I ask a club employee. I remember Ben as a handsome, vibrant man in his early forties. "I'm sorry, Mr. Trump," says the employee, lowering his eyes, "but Mr. Allen died about three years ago."

I then ask about another member, a guy who was always a wonderful companion and a fabulous golfer. "Oh, he's got real problems" is the reply. "In fact, he just went to the hospital for a cancer operation this morning."

Not long after that, a very elderly gentleman shuffles over to me and shakily extends his hand. When he says his name I can't believe what I'm hearing. In my early days at Winged Foot, he'd always struck me as a suave and dapper guy, someone I'd hoped to resemble in my later years. But like a marathoner who suddenly "hits the wall" and starts stumbling, this man appears to have succumbed, all at once, to all the symptoms of old age.

My trip to Winged Foot turned out to be a sobering reminder that everything changes, gradually or—as with my late friends Steve, Mark, and Jon—in the blink of an eye.

PART
II

_____

PART

II

FIVE

RESORTS INTERNATIONAL
Dealing with Merv

MERV Griffin has turned out to be a loyal friend. I know that he's been out there lately, telling everyone, "Watch Donald make the skeptics eat their words." People like him are rare. But Merv and I were once bitter business rivals. In fact, I've always thought that Resorts International was the strangest deal I've ever done. It's working out great for me, and yet, looking back on the whole episode, I'm still not entirely sure why Merv wanted to do business with me in the first place.

Resorts, when it first came to my attention, was a publicly held company that under its founder, Jim Crosby, had experienced success for a while in the hotel-casino business. One of its operations was on Paradise Island in the Bahamas. The company's claim to fame, however, was that it had the first casino ready for customers when gambling came to Atlantic City in 1977. At a time when more cautious businessmen were not investing in land and buildings until they saw if the New Jersey legislature would approve gaming for the area, Crosby—a gruff, smart, chain-smoking Irishman—was buying up property cheaply in the hope that the law would pass. He won his bet—and won big. In those early days of Atlantic City's comeback, gamblers lined up for blocks to get into Resorts. It was still basically the same old Haddon Hall that had been there since the 1920s, a faded lady of a hotel fitted with green felt tables and slot machines. But no one cared, because those who wanted to gamble had no other choice. Resorts, for many months, was the only game in town.

One thing Crosby did with the huge profits he reaped during that period was to bring in Julio Iglesias, Rodney Dangerfield, Don Rickles, and other favorites of the casino crowd and sign them to exclusive long-term contracts. That was a smart move that would give him a competitive edge in entertainment for several years to come. His other big decision—made years later, after hundreds of millions in profits filled the Resorts coffers—was to begin construction of a fantastic state-of-the-art casino-hotel, which would be called the Taj Mahal.

I'm delighted that he did. But I strongly suspect that

when he broke ground for the project, Jim Crosby had no idea what he was in for.

Originally estimated to cost $400 million, the Taj would be the biggest casino-hotel not just in Atlantic City but probably in all of the world. Exactly how big, though, was anyone's guess. As incredible as it sounds, construction had started before the company's inexperienced in-house building unit had finished its plans. I've heard of costs being out of control and jobs falling behind schedule, but this was one project that had no real budget or time frame.

Actually, with or without a plan, it was not a good time for Resorts to be undertaking such a huge project. A lot was happening with the company, and it was virtually all bad. Crosby became increasingly sick and ultimately died of heart failure. The Resorts operation in Atlantic City, once the leading casino in terms of profits, had fallen back in the pack. The Paradise Island operation wasn't doing spectacularly well either.

The Taj, meanwhile, had become an embarrassment. Its construction had been delayed, and convention bookings had been accepted and cancelled so many times that people in the travel business snickered each time another "grand opening" was announced. Some of the contractors hired by Resorts still rattled around inside the huge skeleton of the structure, doing a little electrical work here or putting in sheetrock there. But mostly, the Taj just sat on the Boardwalk, a monument to world-class mismanagement—and to the difficulty of making a truly great dream come true.

It was easy to dismiss Resorts at this point as a total disaster. Most people did. But that only piqued my interest in the company, and I began to do some research. I also contacted a few key members of the Crosby family and began talking to them, in a very preliminary fashion, about the possibility of my taking over Resorts. True, it was in terrible shape, but in business, one man's catastrophe is often another's opportunity. To me, completing the Taj was an opportunity to create the most magnificent casino-hotel in Atlantic City—or perhaps the world.

One thing I found out as I began to look into the possibility of buying Resorts was that Jack Pratt, the head of the Pratt Hotels Corporation, had called on the company shortly after the death of its founder. The Crosby family, which retained a controlling interest in the company, wanted to sell out as soon as possible. But Pratt's deal had stalled.

Marvin Davis also took a run at Resorts around this time. His complicated offer would have allowed him to strip away the Paradise Island operation and leave the company with all its other problems. The Resorts board rejected Davis's plan as not in the company's best interest.

I personally found dealing with the Crosby family a pleasant experience. They were totally honorable people. As soon as I expressed an interest in Resorts, they forgot about Davis and Pratt and began working with me to find a way to make a deal happen. After all, I had both the means to take the troubled company off their hands and the desire to salvage Jim Crosby's grander schemes and dreams. And this was at a time when the family wasn't exactly being besieged with viable offers.

It was easy to see why the world wasn't beating a path to Resorts' door. The company was unusual in several ways. First, there was the A-B stock structure. Long before I came along, Resorts had set up a system that involved two classes of stock. The Class A stock traded publicly and, like all stock, represented equity in the company. But the A shares had very little voting power. The Class B stock, on the other hand, constituted less than 10 percent of the company's equity, but it had voting superiority over the A stock of one hundred to one. What this meant, essentially, was that the Crosby family, by virtue of owning almost all of the B stock, could control the company without having to buy up most of the outstanding shares.

My interest was in running Resorts, not merely investing in it. So I wanted the B stock. After negotiating with the Crosby family's representatives, I arranged to purchase approximately 750,000 Class B shares, or about 90 percent of what was available, from the family for $135 a share. That was much more than the A shares traded for, but I was paying a premium for voting control. As the CEO of Resorts, I'd still have to answer to a board of directors, half of whom were from outside the Trump Organization. But at just over $100 million, the deal, I felt instinctively, was a decent one.

Compared with what the numbers would have been years earlier, that price seemed bargain-basement. But Resorts in 1987 bore little resemblance to the company as it existed a few years before Crosby died. Back then, the annual report listed $300 million in cash and no debt. When I took over, the company had $740 million in debt and little cash.

That swing of more than $1 billion can be traced back to various mistakes. Jim Crosby, an entrepreneur who owed much to casinos, became obsessed instead with real estate, investing huge amounts of money in buying up overpriced bits and strips of property in every corner of Atlantic City. He also indulged his passion for aviation in several expensive ways. One bad move involved his purchase of Pan Am stock at a most inopportune time; the company eventually had to sell its shares at a $50 million loss. But that investment seems solid compared with his $50 million stake in a fleet of specially equipped seaplanes, which were supposed to scoop water out of rivers and lakes and dump it on forest fires. He called these aircraft Albatrosses, and with good reason. For years the planes just sat rusting someplace in the Arizona desert, and the last I heard they were still there.

Crosby, once a brilliant investor, also lost a bundle on the commodities market, and $30 million more on what was supposed to be a state-of-the-art shrimp farm. But what really broke my heart, as a builder and businessman, was what had happened with the Taj.

Going back over his records and partial plans, I could see that Crosby once had dared to dream of one of the most fantastic structures the world had ever seen. His idea was breathtaking, but pulling it off was another matter. By the time I took control of the company, nearly $500 million had been spent, and the Taj was nowhere near completion.

The files told a story of money running out and fear setting in. The size of the hotel's casino, for example, had been changed several times, from 120,000 to 60,000 to 100,000 square feet, as the Resorts people lost confidence in their instincts and began changing their minds frequently for no good reason. In the beginning, everything about the Taj had been first-class. As time went on, however, there had been many self-defeating cutbacks and compromises. The latest plans called for a drastically shrunken-down casino and total elimination of the lavish high-roller suites that were needed to attract key customers. Tacky light fixtures would replace chandeliers, and instead of beautifully beveled mirrors on the walls, Resorts was calling for cheap vinyl coverings. Even more incredible was the decision to open only two of the twelve proposed restaurants. What this meant was that a hotel promoting itself as the ultimate in luxury and convenience wouldn't even have a place where people could comfortably eat.

Whipping the Taj into shape, I knew, was going to take huge amounts of time, energy, and skill, not to mention my ability to secure additional financing. I never doubted for a moment that I could get the place up and running. What I couldn't see was how, in my salaried position as chairman of Resorts, I could ever be fairly compensated for transforming an already legendary disaster into a winner.

My solution to this problem was to ask the Resorts board for a management contract. Under my plan, the Trump Organization would receive 3 percent of the Taj's construction costs and 1.75 percent of the gross revenues of Resorts, as well as about 15 percent of the profits. In deference to the company's poor financial condition, I said I would waive any payment on the contract until the Taj was completed and generating cash.

Because it was an unusual idea that involved some potentially big numbers, I knew the management contract would need to get approval from all the outside directors, as well as from independent financial and legal experts. But I decided to be bold and present the proposal anyway. It would then be up to all of them to decide if I was worth it.

Not surprisingly, the outside directors and their experts debated the idea, then debated it some more. In fact, they gave the proposal exhaustive consideration. They approved it and it went to the Casino Control Commission for even more discussion. In short, a collection of many minds was doing its usual thing. In the meantime, I knew that if Resorts was to survive, I'd better hurry up and do mine. This meant getting a loan of $125 million from a New Jersey bank, which probably wouldn't even have considered such financing if I hadn't come aboard. I also had to address quickly a technical matter—apparently overlooked by the former Resorts management—which could have scuttled the whole Taj construction.

My brother Robert and Harvey Freeman had discovered, while checking out paperwork related to the project, that one half of the land beneath the hotel was designated as urban renewal property. Under the agreement that had been struck with Resorts, that parcel would revert to the Atlantic City Housing Authority if construction of the Taj was not finished by February 1988. Although Resorts was obviously going to miss that deadline by a mile, no one from the company had so much as requested a meeting with the city to discuss an extension. Resorts, moreover, had managed to get itself embroiled in a lawsuit with the local government over an unrelated matter. Clearly, it was time to start talking to city officials. The people at the housing authority, once we sat down and explained our situation, were as shocked as I'd been to learn about the chaos within the company. In a matter of days they granted us an extension of the original agreement.

I loved the idea of being able to wade into a major construction project as badly botched as the Taj and make instant improvements. The Taj plan, for example, called for a private elevator to run from Crosby's large apartment on the top floor to the lobby, with no stops in between. It was, I suppose, one way for a man who wanted to disassociate himself from the throngs to come and go without so much as seeing his own customers. Yet it also stuck out as a tremendous waste of money and construction time. I kept the elevator but transformed the apartment into an elaborate two-bedroom suite, a place fit for the kind of player who's capable of winning or losing four or five million dollars in a single weekend.

Then I moved on to the next disaster—a set of too-skinny escalators that were being built so narrow because prior management believed people moving between floors don't stand side by side. "Maybe they were right," I said to Mark Etess, who was then the president of the Taj. "But these things look silly. Let's rip 'em out."

Anyone, of course, could have torn the place apart and started all over again. The key was knowing what *not* to change. For example, the Taj was originally designed to have a beautiful 120,000-square-foot casino, by far the largest in the world. No other hotel in Atlantic City could offer that kind of space. It would be perfect for accommodating huge crowds, which the town could never handle before. I wouldn't have changed it for the world.

"Taj Mahal" is a perfect name because it suggests glamour and mystery in three wonderfully soft syllables. Creating the right image is the key to success in the casino business or any other business, and that vital process starts with the name. I added "Trump" to the name, just as I use "Trump" on the Plaza, the Castle, and the Regency, because it's always been a great marketing tool. But pick the wrong name, and no matter what else you do, you'll never be a hit.

One thing I've learned about the construction business—and life in general—is that while *what* you do is obviously important, the most important thing is just to *do something*. You can waste tremendous amounts of time agonizing over which course of action to take when, in fact, any of the choices you're considering is probably preferable to continued pondering, which only heightens your fear of making a mistake. Consider the example of General George B. McClellan, the head of the Union army during the early stages of the Civil War. Not wanting to spoil his perfect record, McClellan prepared for battle endlessly but was never in the mood to fight. This cost him some key victories and eventually his command. McClellanitis seems to be a trait embedded deep within human nature. Think of how the Resorts guys were vacillating about the size of the Taj's casino. Should it be 60,000 or 80,000 square feet? As soon as I took charge, I said, "We're going to build it at 120,000 square feet—the maximum and the best." Did I make precisely the right move? I hope so, but I really don't know. What I do understand is that sizing the casino in a major hotel is not an exact science. All you can do is decide what you think makes sense—and then move on to the next challenge.

Being decisive also motivates the troops. In my line, that often means contractors and their crews—not a terribly impressionable lot, normally, unless you happen to be a beautiful woman in a tight skirt walking by on their lunch hour. When I assumed control of Resorts, all previous arrangements with building tradesmen were automatically cancelled—which was perfect, as far as I was concerned. I wanted to wipe the slate clean and forge a whole new set of relationships with the electricians, carpenters, plasterers, and other tradespeople who'd be working on the Taj. Because my father was a builder, I grew up with these people and know them well. Contractors are a breed apart—extremely street-smart and independent, often wealthier than many famous Wall Street financiers, but interested only in having the biggest house in their section of Queens or Staten Island. Show a strong contractor a hint of weakness, and you haven't got a chance. These are, don't forget, basically the same bunch of guys who make a fortune off New York City by building Second Avenue subway tunnels to nowhere and charging "extras" that end up costing millions. But approach them with a combination of firmness and fairness and you'll get your building up according to plan.

I knew I'd done a good job of selecting and motivating my contractors and workmen when I visited the construction site early one morning and one of them yelled at me angrily, "For Christ's sake, Mr. Trump, watch where the f—you're going." At first I couldn't believe what I was hearing. Then I realized that I had inadvertently stepped on a corner of the casino underfloor that he'd just painted. On some jobs I've seen, the workmen didn't give a damn what happened; they were just there to collect their hourly wage. But this guy had fire and pride. He cared. And if he did, so, probably, did the others. Under those circumstances, obscenity is music to my ears. As Abraham Lincoln said about the often-cantankerous General McClellan, "I would gladly hold his horse if he would only win my war for me."

By December 1987, several months after I submitted the proposal, both the Resorts board and the Casino Control Commission had approved my management contract. I'd made, or changed, all the key design decisions by that time. And construction on the Taj—which had finally been stabilized at 4,000,000 square feet, or only a little smaller than the Pentagon—was going smoothly.

I should have been deliriously happy. But something gnawed at me, and I knew what it was—the whole head-of-a-public-company routine. Although I certainly agreed with the theory of stockholder-owned corporations and was absolutely committed to fulfilling my fiduciary duties, I personally didn't like answering to a board of directors. I could have lived with that, but the stock market crash of October 1987 completely changed the financial picture. Suddenly, resorts financing sources dried up.

The only way to make sense of the situation, I soon decided, was to buy up a majority of the outstanding A shares through a tender offer and take the company private. The price I came up with, based on my knowledge of Resorts, was $15.00 a share. Since the company's A shares had traded publicly for around $11.50 following the stock market crash two months earlier, I thought it was a reasonable offer. The Resorts board's independent directors disagreed, though, and we negotiated upward. My final offer was $22.00 a share, or almost double the market value. They and their financial and legal experts thought that was fair.

As soon as you file a tender offer—especially one that involves taking a company private—a lot of things start happening. All sorts of Securities and Exchange

Commission reports have to be completed and sent out, while at the same time, stockholder lawsuits calling the tender offer scandalously inadequate begin, predictably, to trickle in. I remember saying to Susan Heilbron, who was my chief in-house attorney and handled many of my SEC-related matters, that I was amazed at how quickly people file suits and how similarly their documents are worded. "That's because it's just a bunch of legal boilerplate, stored on word processors," she said. "As soon as a tender offer is filed, the computers whir, and these things go out automatically." (This is a disgrace. If the losers had to pay the cost of lawsuits in this country, you would reduce the caseloads of the overworked judiciary by 75 percent.)

It soon became apparent, though, that one thing *was* unusual about the response to my offer. A lot of the static was coming from Merv Griffin.

At the time I knew only one thing about Merv the businessman. It was that he had sold the rights to several of the game shows he produced to Coca-Cola for the much-ballyhooed sum of $250 million.

Although, as I said, I now regard Merv as a friend, my initial contacts with him were less than impressive. Actually, they were more like noncontacts. Instead of calling me up directly, the way a Carl Icahn or a Bob Bass would have done in a similar situation, and saying, "Look, Donald, I want Resorts too," Merv put off any man-to-man confrontation. He preferred to talk through his lawyers. Over the Dow Jones wire one day came word that he had filed a suit challenging Resorts' two-tier stock system. At about the same time he also made a roundabout effort to force the company to issue more B stock, which he intended to buy up. We'd win both those battles easily, my lawyers said. Resorts was hardly the only company with a two-tier system, and no one could order us to issue stock. Still, they warned me, if Merv wanted to, he could tie us up in court and ruin our timetable for the Taj.

One thing I'll say about Merv is that he's taken to heart that old show-biz adage about always having to top yourself. His shtick definitely got wilder as he went along. When he made his own tender offer for the outstanding Resorts A shares, his bid was $35.00 a share. That's $13.00 more per share than I was offering for a stock recently trading at about $11.50.

By this time I'd learned that Merv was being guided in the Resorts deal by New York lawyers who had no personal financial stake in the success of a deal. Their interest was in trying to match buyers with sellers and taking a cut of the action from whichever party they happened to represent. My guess is that to make the deal go, some of Merv's advisers very smartly played on his ego, telling him how sweet it would feel to steal this company away from Donald Trump.

But while I can make an educated guess as to why the advisers might have encouraged Griffin to go forward, I don't know to this day why Merv offered

$35.00 a share for the Resorts stock. Remember, all he needed to do to top me was to bid $23.00. Or $22.50. Usually, as I've said, I have a sense of what's motivating the other guy in a deal. But any way I looked at Merv's move, it didn't figure. Though I'm not really litigious by today's standards, I had no choice but to sue him for interfering with my tender offer. Merv countersued—a reaction that is expected in such situations.

Later that same day I called Merv and extended a cordial invitation for him to drop by my office the next time he was in town. He, sounding equally genial, said it just so happened he'd be in New York in a few days, and he'd like to do just that.

Merv's air of relaxed cheerfulness on the phone didn't surprise me. It was all part of the dealmaker's dance. The way I looked at it, if he wanted to get into all the posturing and maneuvering that seem to be part of even the most mundane transactions these days, that was fine with me.

I was prepared for anything—except Merv's entrance into my office. Although much heavier than in his TV days, he looked to me as if he had just come off the set. I was expecting him to say something about it, but he didn't; he just sat there smiling and nodding while we got to know each other, one-on-one, over the course of the next hour.

In the *60 Minutes* segment that Mike Wallace would later do about the deal, Merv said that he had cunningly used his skills as a talk-show host to draw me out during this initial discussion. Well, I certainly did do most of the talking. And I hoped Merv was listening because I gave him an honest appraisal of the hotel-casinos he seemed so desperately to covet.

The Paradise Island and the Atlantic City Resorts facilities were, I told him, merely treading water. In order to be profitable, they needed, in my opinion, a minimum of $150 million in improvements. "If you're pursuing a takeover," I said to him, "you have to ask yourself now if you're able and willing to make that kind of commitment." The Taj, I told him, was a very different story. It could be the most fabulous facility of its kind. But was Merv prepared to invest another $600 million or so in a hotel that had already cost its previous owner about that much? As a guy who'd never built anything bigger than a *Wheel of Fortune* set, did he feel prepared to deal with the contractors, unions, bureaucrats, and politicians who stood between him and success?

What I wanted to do was present the reality of the situation without embellishment. The facts, in this case, spoke eloquently for themselves. The first thing they said was that Resorts, as currently constituted, was a huge burden to assume. The Taj Mahal had taken one management down into a mire of debt, and it stood there, half-finished, waiting to take down Merv. The other truth I hoped to convey was that the challenge of successfully finishing and owning the Taj

"If you say so," I said. "But any fool could take me on, Mike. Suppose I told you that Merv has the media bamboozled?"

"If we find that," Mike said, "I promise, you'll see it on the screen."

And so, on a Sunday night in early 1989, America did see it. I thought the *60 Minutes* piece portrayed the situation accurately. Despite his background as a TV personality, Merv didn't do especially well on camera, particularly in the later scenes, which were filmed after the Atlantic City and Bahamas hotels had been folded into the Griffin Company. Mike Wallace felt obliged to mention Merv's shaky demeanor. I, on the other hand, was finally getting the freedom to tell my side of the Resorts story (much as I will soon be telling the current story).

I had made numerous one-dollar bets with people in my organization who didn't think I could keep my mouth shut while Merv got all the glory, and I had collected from them all with glee. But then, just as the deal was getting set to close, a reporter from *Business Week* wrote a detailed story which carried the headline DONALD TEACHES MERV THE ART OF THE DEAL. As it turned out, Merv, still hellbent on buying his hotels, didn't have much to say about the story. But the Casino Control Commission, after seeing the facts laid out in the national media, decided that Merv's company needed to get more money for the Taj so that he could reduce his debt burden. In the end, I agreed to add $25 million to the purchase price. Merv also had to put up more of his own money so that he'd need to borrow less.

This was one of those deals that have to be nursed along to the finish line. Early on, for instance, I decided, as a matter of strategy, to fight Merv on some relatively minor points, such as who would get a couple of helicopters and several billboards that belonged to Resorts as we divided the company's assets. Negotiations actually stalled several times over these smaller points. But that was okay; a little acrimony in such situations is only normal. In the end, Harvey Freeman, who was handling the more detailed aspects of the negotiations for me, would usually back off and let Merv win, a tactic that tended to keep him happy and always moving forward toward the eventual signing. (But on many other points I would not back down, even if it meant blowing the deal. You must always be prepared to walk—and mean it.)

Some developments did worry me, though, starting with the fact that Merv was getting his financing through Drexel Burnham at a time when that firm was becoming increasingly preoccupied with Mike Milken and associated problems. The Casino Control Commission, meanwhile, seemed less than enamored of something in the past of the Griffin Company's president, Mike Nigris, the guy Harvey Freeman was dealing with on a day-to-day basis. Since the deal was predicated on Merv's getting licensed, I was deeply concerned—until the day Susan Heilbron told me that Nigris had "disappeared himself" for the sake of the company. Only in the casino business can the guy you were negotiating with one day become a missing person the next. Except for one brief sighting of Nigris crossing Fifth Avenue about a year later, reported by a member of my staff, no one I know has seen the guy since.

Ego. That's probably the only way to explain The Deal That Made No Sense. Certainly *something* was preventing Merv, a sharp guy, from truly seeing the numbers that people kept placing in his path. I laid out the facts for him in our very first meeting. Mike Wallace asked Merv on camera if he understood that his debt-service payments would be exceeding his income by $109,000 a day. And the Casino Control Commission kept reminding Merv during his licensing process that he was saddling himself with $925 million in long-term debt. His reply, right up until he signed the Resorts deal, was "Hey, don't worry. I can handle those kinds of numbers." He even told the Casino Control Commission, "I want the record to show that the takeover I'm making is a hostile takeover." In other words, he wrested the company from a kicking-and-screaming Donald Trump.

At one time Merv had criticized me and tried to mock me for putting my name on my Atlantic City hotels. Late in 1989, however, he announced that he was changing the name of Resorts International to

Merv Griffin's Resorts. A new advertising campaign was launched and renovations on the old building were begun. None of those things worked as well as the Griffin people hoped, and in December 1989 the company sought bankruptcy protection.

The Taj, meanwhile, opened on April 4, 1990, right on time. I have a great love for all fabulous structures, but the Taj blows me away. It's a marvelous facility, from the jewel-encrusted casino to the elaborate high-roller suites on the tower's top floor.

Merv had the grace to speak at the opening of the Taj, which shows that despite our problems, he feels that I treated him fairly. The bitterness between us is gone. It's time now for me to thank Merv publicly for giving me the opportunity to do what he never wanted to—make the Taj a reality.

My confirmation in June 1959. I'm in the back row, second from the right.

With Ted
Turner and
friends in
October 1988.

Michael
Douglas and
me in 1988.

With Malcolm Forbes before our falling-out.

Don Johnson and I share a passion for speedboat racing.

The wrestler Hulk Hogan is a great showman. (I'm standing on a box.)

Michael Jackson and me, on the opening weekend at the Taj Mahal. (this time, I'm kneeling.)

Two of my new friends, Mike Tyson and Merv Griffin.

Sugar Ray Leonard is a superb boxer.

With George and Barbara Bush during the 1988 presidential campaign.

Benazir Bhutto, the prime minister of Pakistan, and me during her New York visit in 1988.

Mike Wallace, Merv Griffin, and me, during our 1989 *60 Minutes* bout.

Mayor Ed Koch, Tony Gliedman, vice president of the Trump Organization, and I open the Lasker ice-skating rink in Central Park, my second for the city.

Ivana and me in better days.

VOGUE

MAY $3.00

SUMMER FASHION SPECIAL

cool whites

hot prints

dress for less:
sporting chic

women & cholesterol:
the real story

IVANA TRUMP'S
WINNING STYLE

Ivana on a recent cover of *Vogue* magazine.

The Plaza Hotel.

The Trump Shuttle is now the best airline of its kind anywhere.

The *Trump Princess* is probably the most beautiful yacht ever built. But it was more trophy than personal toy.

The fabulous Taj Mahal, under construction and finished.

My trusted associates and close friends.

Stephen F. Hyde, CEO of my Trump Atlantic City properties.

SIX

GRAND HO

The Plaza
Purchase

EVER since I got out of college, I've
of ten New York properties that I
quire. I'm not ready to reveal wh
But I will say that the Plaza Hotel has a
number one on that list.

Actually, the Plaza has intrigued me si
kid. Maybe it was because I thought it
French castle or because horse-drawn h
were parked across the street near Centra
way, I've always been captivated by that
building at Fifty-ninth and Fifth.

I didn't have any personal involveme
hotel, though, until I began buying stock i
Corporation in early 1987. Allegis, on

d Airlines, owned the Westin Hotel chain, which
t time included the Plaza.

njoyed being connected, even in that indirect way,
the great hotel. But that's really not why I bought
stock. I liked Allegis because I thought it was
orming far below its potential. As an investor, I'll
ays look twice at a company that has great assets
lousy management.

ake, for example, the decision to drop the name
ted Airlines in favor of Allegis. I considered that
uly dumb move, and I wasn't shy about calling
hard Ferris, who was then the company's CEO,
telling him how I felt. "Why would you even
sider doing such a thing?" I once asked him. "You
e one of the best corporate names there are. Every
e someone mentions United Airlines, you're getting
licity for your core business. Why would you spend
ty-five or forty million dollars to change all your
os, all over the world, to a name that means nothing
nybody?"

erris defended the decision by saying something
ut "show-casing the new corporate synergy." I
ned awhile, then said, "Look, in my opinion the
d 'Allegis' should be reserved for the next great
ase."

few days later I repeated that remark publicly.
only did reporters use it in articles, but it wound
ppearing in many newspapers as the Quote of the
k. When Ferris was finally forced out not long

Mark Grossinger Etess, from the famous hotel family, president of the Taj Mahal.

Jonathan Benanav, senior vice president, operations, Trump Plaza Hotel and Casino.

afterward, a lot of people said that the "disease" crack brought about his fall. That could be. All I know is that the quote came at the right time, and it focused attention on the fact that something was seriously wrong.

The Plaza served as further proof of Allegis's careless management, if anyone needed it. Ever since it was built, in 1907, the hotel had been a monument to success and glamour. The Vanderbilts, Wanamakers, and Whitneys had stayed in its luxurious suites and sipped champagne with visiting royalty in the Grand Ballroom. But after about thirty years as a corporation-owned hotel, the Plaza looked tired and shabby. Anyone could see the effect of years of neglect in the lobby, where the carpets were getting worn, and in the Palm Court, where the flowers always looked a little faded. Previous owners had even closed down what had been the Rose Room, and later the Persian Room, and leased it to a nondescript dress store at a ridiculously low rate.

I would have loved to get my hands on the Plaza and use my management skills to return the hotel to its former stature. I happen to have a good track record with New York City hotels. The transformation of the old Commodore into the magnificent Grand Hyatt was a key deal early in my career, and since then I'd revitalized the St. Moritz, on Central Park South and Sixth Avenue. Still, I didn't waste time daydreaming about the possibility of owning the Plaza. For one thing, its corporate ownership made that unfeasible. For another, my investment in Allegis was then going through the roof as others began realizing the asset value of the company. That development left me with two options: I could hold on to my shares and retain my remote connection with the Plaza, or I could sell the stock and make a huge profit after just a few months. It was not exactly a tough decision. I sold the stock.

What happened next surprised me. Just as I was turning my attention from Allegis, the company announced that as part of a huge restructuring plan, it was selling off all of its nonairline assets, including, of course, the Plaza.

That definitely piqued my interest, but only to a point. The Plaza, I realized, would be coming on the market as part of the sixty-one-hotel Westin chain. To get the one property I wanted, I'd have to buy the whole package and then spend at least a year or two selling off the sixty hotels that I couldn't care less about. To make matters even less appealing, as far as I was concerned, Allegis had decided to conduct an auction for the Westin chain. As a guy who prefers to negotiate one-on-one, I'll usually drop out of a deal rather than participate in an auction.

This time, though, when a representative from First Boston—the company Westin had hired to run the sale—contacted me, I agreed, albeit warily, to participate. I figured that the auction process would bring a price considerably higher than I wanted to pay. Still, it didn't cost anything to make a bid, and by being part of the process, I'd no doubt get to know more about the Plaza and the people who were in the market to buy it.

The rules First Boston planned to go by were especially elaborate. Instead of having one auction, there would be a weeding-out process whereby selected potential buyers would make a preliminary bid that would, if high enough, qualify them for the final auction some six weeks later. My preliminary bid was $1.3 billion. That, as it turned out, placed me in the middle of a pack of potential buyers that included Marvin Davis, the Kuwaiti government, and the team of Bob Bass and John Aoki.

It was the highest bid I'd ever made in my career, but it meant nothing. The serious moves in the deal, I knew, had yet to be made. And when they started, anything could happen.

The buying and selling of world-class hotels is an emotional business. When a place like the Plaza is on the block, the toughest negotiators become soft, and logic often gets tossed out the window. Study the recent market and you'll see the sultan of Brunei buying the Beverly Hills Hotel at an unrealistic figure, a Japanese group paying a huge price for the Intercontinental chain, and numerous other examples of people getting carried away when it comes to hotel purchases. Actually, the value of many things comes down to emotion. Why else are people paying $400 an ounce for gold and hundreds of thousands of dollars for a diamond that has absolutely no practical value? But hotels can arouse passions faster than any other possessions. When major ones come on the market, potential buyers start fantasizing about bringing their friends there, owning the social center of a community, and making the ultimate personal statement. The result is often a price with no basis in reality.

Just when everyone's emotions could be expected to kick in, I decided to drop out. After reviewing the detailed financial information that Allegis made available to the auction "finalists," I concluded that as much as I loved the Plaza, the circumstances just weren't right. When the time came, I would put in an unrealistically low bid of $1 billion for the Westin chain and leave it at that.

In dealmaking, you have to be able to draw a line and say to yourself, This is as far as I'm going. The ability to do that is in the genes; either you have it or you don't. I know a guy who's a Wharton graduate and has a truly brilliant business mind—when he works for other people. But a few months ago he was buying a house for himself, and he was a total disaster. "Don, what should I do?" he'd say to me. "Should I call the broker, the owner? My God, what's happening with this house?" He hadn't slept for about a week. I told him, "You know, you're really lucky you work for someone else, as opposed to being your own guy, because emotionally you're not equipped to be your own boss.'' The true deal people sleep at night no matter what.

In any case, no sooner had I decided to drop out of the auction than I got a phone call from a talented lawyer named Tom Barrack, asking if he might stop by my office to chat about the Plaza situation. At that time I didn't know much about Barrack, except that he represented Bob Bass, a Texas oil magnate and investor who was starting to emerge from the shadow of his older brother, Sid. I'd done business with Bob a few years earlier, when he sold me his 21 percent interest in the Alexander's retail chain for $50 million, and I liked his style. His approach to the Westin auction was no exception. Bob, with Tom Barrack's help, had hooked up with John Aoki, the head of a huge Tokyo-based construction firm, for the express purpose of acquiring Westin. Since Bob was interested mainly in the Plaza, and Aoki was excited by the prospect of owning a coast-to-coast American chain, it looked like an ideal partnership. In the upcoming auction, they seemed the team to beat.

It was obvious that Tom agreed with my assessment when he came by for our get-to-know-you session. But as he sat across the desk from me, exuding confidence and exchanging pleasantries, he also seemed to be subtly probing to see how I might feel about buying the Plaza if Bob Bass acquired it and then decided for some reason to sell. That could easily have been taken as a sign of fear or indecision on Bass's part. But I saw it as something else: a very shrewd, very conservative businessman making sure he had a back door out of his deal if he wanted it.

My response was immediate and straightforward. "Tom, if you ever find yourself wanting to sell the Plaza," I said, "consider me interested." There was no reason to be cute or coy. I didn't want to pick up the paper one day and find out the Plaza had been sold to some sheik or Far Eastern conglomerate. At the same time, there was no reason for him to know that the hotel was, in fact, number one on my secret wishlist.

A few days after Tom Barrack and I had our meeting, in mid-October of 1987, the stock market crashed, dropping five hundred points in a single afternoon. One thing this did was make a shambles of the upcoming Westin auction. Hoping that First Boston might be feeling a little panicky and jump at any halfway decent offer, many of the would-be buyers started making preemptive bids. One group, headed by former Westin CEO Harry Mulliken, offered just over $1 billion, and Marvin Davis weighed in at $1.15 billion. When the dust settled, though, it was Bass and Aoki who had walked away with the Westin chain for a reported $1.53 billion.

I was glad to see that happen. From the start, Bob Bass, the chairman of the National Trust for Historic Preservation, loved the Plaza as only a connoisseur of fine buildings could. Soon after the deal closed, he and his wife, Anne, came in from Fort Worth and spent some time at the hotel, walking through the corridors and having dinner in the Oak Room. (Bob's brother, Sid, would later get married at the Plaza.) By then, I'd all but put the Plaza out of my mind. I was too busy with other deals to feel bad.

And then Barrack called again.

On the phone his tone was as charming and non-committal as ever, but his suggestion that we get together for a breakfast meeting made me think that Bob and John Aoki must be contemplating a move of some kind. I'd always thought that they might consider selling off the crown jewel of the Westin chain, the Plaza, because, if handled properly, that could in effect reduce by about $400 million the rather full price they'd paid for the chain, and make the Westin acquisition more reasonable. Over breakfast, however, Barrack insisted that Bob was too enthralled with the Plaza to sell. Although I liked Tom Barrack a lot, I wanted to say, "Well, then, what the hell are we doing here eating croissants?"

What I did instead was pepper him with questions that I wanted him to take back to his group: Had Bob really thought about life with New York's tough hotel unions? What about the Plaza's outdated computer and phone systems? Had he considered the need to replace the freight elevators still working on the 1907 water hydraulic machinery? Did he really think he could manage a property like this from Texas? I was emphatic, but friendly. If Barrack wanted to arrange a sale, he knew where to come. If not, life would go on.

After that, several weeks went by in which I was busy doing a lot of things, including last-minute work on a boxing match between Mike Tyson and the former heavyweight champ Larry Holmes. I sensed it shaping up as a huge success—a night in which the Atlantic City convention center would be packed with celebrities such as Madonna, Don Johnson, Norman Mailer, and John McEnroe—and so I invited Barrack to fly down with me in my helicopter. I wanted to keep in touch with Tom, whom I liked personally, but more than that, I wanted him to understand that I would definitely not be overwhelmed by the prospect of owning the world's greatest hotel.

It was an important point to communicate. When you're in the position to sell a truly precious piece of real estate, you don't deal with just anyone who has the money; you look for the kind of people who will cherish the property and bring something to it by their very presence.

On the night of the fight I introduced Barrack to a lot of people, half kiddingly, as "a guy I'm going to be doing a very big deal with." It was part positive thinking on my part and, because the line was a little presumptuous, and Barrack knew it, part private joke. I kept up that friendly bantering tone whenever we spoke on the phone during the next couple of months. It wasn't anything terribly calculated, but it worked to relieve the tension between two parties who probably were thinking about each other a lot but saying very little in each other's presence. In a deal you never want to be tough or unfriendly for no reason. You can often get a lot more accomplished—and besides, life is just plain more pleasant—when you deal as friends instead of enemies.

In January 1988 Tom Barrack called and suggested we have another meeting. When he mentioned that David Bonderman, Bob Bass's chief of staff, happened to be in New York and would like to sit in on the discussion, I agreed. Maybe, I thought, after all these months, they were finally ready to make a move. The meeting, though, turned out to be a total dud. I sensed Bonderman was a testy guy the minute I saw him, but I explained that I understood very well the difficulty of running a hotel from a great distance, as well as their desire to get a fair price. I also made a pitch for myself as a guy who was in a financial position not only to close the deal immediately but also to carry off the major renovation the building deserved. They listened, then said that Bob Bass didn't see being based in Texas as an insurmountable problem, and in any case, the Plaza really wasn't for sale. It was the same frustrating stuff I'd been hearing for months. Bonderman was especially discouraging, and after the discussion had broken up, I asked Jonathan Bernstein, an attorney of mine who'd sat in with me that day, "What did you make of all that?" Jon shook his head and said, "It went from looking good to not looking good awful fast." I had to agree. But then, that wasn't surprising. Almost every deal is a bit of a roller-coaster ride; you've got to realize that at the outset and just relax.

About two weeks after that get-together, Barrack called, quite out of the blue, and said he'd like to have another meeting—to discuss the possible sale of the Plaza. This time I *was* surprised, but I put off feeling happy about the sudden development until I heard their price.

When he arrived in my office, Barrack was as polite as ever, but very businesslike. Bob Bass would accept no less than $450 million in cash for the hotel, he said. Then he added that if I was interested, I'd have to agree to waive the standard contingency clause. That would represent a huge concession on my part because if I waived that clause, and anything in the financial data or in the building itself proved faulty or not as promised, I couldn't sue.

On the whole, though, it was an interesting proposal. Barrack's price wasn't as outrageous as it might have been. The Plaza, if you considered its stature, its history, and its attractiveness to the kind of buyer to whom money is no object, was worth that much or more. On the other hand, if you looked at the situation strictly in economic terms, comparing the cash flow the hotel generated with the annual financing charges that would be due, $450 million was a high price.

I wasn't going to be a fool for love, I told Barrack. The way I saw things, $350 million was the right price. He didn't register any particular emotion, but since we didn't even seem to be within haggling distance, there was nothing to do but shake hands and part company. By the time he got on the elevator, I was knee-deep in other important business.

I'm not by any means a workaholic, as I've said, but having a lot on your plate is one of the golden secrets of dealmaking. I'll never forget a friend who once spent two years concentrating on a single big project. "There's no way you can make a good deal," I told him. "When the heavy negotiating starts, you'll be thinking about what you have at stake and how it might all go to waste, and the other side will see the fear in your eyes and take advantage of you." To make sure I don't ever find myself in that position, I try to have a minimum of ten deals working at all times. That way I can concentrate on the ones that are going well and walk away from the rest.

Which is exactly what I did after that meeting with Barrack.

It wasn't easy knowing that perhaps the one chance I'd ever have to own the Plaza might be slipping through my fingers, but I put the hotel out of my mind and resisted the temptation to go anywhere near it. If I had been seen walking around the Plaza at this point,

I would not only have given Barrack a chance to see how interested I was, I would also have drawn out the sharks who come out of nowhere and drive up the price of anything I'm after on the theory that if Trump wants it, it must be worth having. So although it's my style to research a property thoroughly, I stayed far away. People in my organization—people who remembered that when I was buying an apartment house in Brooklyn or Queens I would check out every screw and bolt—would say to me, "How is the piping? What about the air conditioning?" And I would have to say, "Look, we'll check all that out after we close. This is the Plaza Hotel I'm buying, and the Plaza Hotel is much more than the sum of its parts."

Tom Barrack and I didn't talk for the next three weeks. Then on Saturday, February 27, I called Tom and asked if he could come by my office the following Tuesday morning.

I just sensed in my gut that it was time to get the deal done—for several reasons. I knew Bob Bass didn't need to sell the Plaza for financial purposes, yet it was clear that he was actively looking for a buyer. Barrack, I knew, had been talking to a number of investors from all over the world, including Australia and Hong Kong. I'm sure they were all fine people, but the Plaza, after years of neglect, deserved something better than absentee ownership and ordinary management. Here I was, meanwhile, a guy with a vision of what the hotel could be and the money to make that vision a reality. In all honesty, I could have delayed more and negotiated harder for the Plaza; normally I believe in fighting all-out for every point. But this was a unique situation. In my mind it was simply right and proper for me to have the Plaza. For Bob Bass to sell to anyone else, I felt, would have just been plain silly.

My Tuesday meeting with Barrack lasted about ten minutes. Essentially, we met halfway between our original offers, at $400 million, and had an agreement to protect the deal while my lawyer Jon Bernstein and Barrack worked out the details. Two weeks later we reconvened to hash things out more definitely. After thinking about it, Barrack said Bob Bass thought the price should be $10 million more than what we'd agreed on. I agreed to go to $407.5 million but asked that the deal now include 22 Central Park South, an apartment building next door to the Plaza. I also asked for the reinstatement of the contingency clause so I'd have legal recourse in the event of any major problems. Barrack agreed to those points.

The sale of the Plaza was a huge news event. No one had ever paid more for a single hotel, and the immediate reaction from the Monday-morning quarterbacks was that I'd greatly overpaid. Some people even compared me with Merv Griffin, saying that I'd gotten carried away much as he had in the Resorts deal and that I wasn't my usual self. To that I can only say that I wound up with the Plaza. I was so happy to have it that I was delighted with the deal I'd made. Tom and Bob Bass were totally honorable. I know that while the contracts were being prepared they got several offers for substantially more money than I was paying, and from some very powerful groups. But they refused even to accept these people's phone calls. Their integrity reminded me a lot of the time when I was setting out to build Trump Tower and was negotiating with Walter Hoving, the president of Tiffany, for the crucial air rights over his building. When his subordinates came to him and said, "We can get more money than Trump is paying," Walter was incredulous. "You don't understand," he said. "I gave my word. I shook his hand." Bob Bass, John Aoki, and Tom Barrack were exactly the same way. In a world full of deceit and dishonor, it's nice to know such people exist.

I trusted Tom and the others so implicitly that I began spending time and money on the Plaza even before the deal officially closed. That's something I wouldn't normally do, if only because hotel closings can be complicated all-night affairs in which teams of lawyers and accountants from both sides argue over exactly what's included in the purchase price. I'll never forget the situation with Leona Helmsley in 1985, when I bought the St. Moritz from her husband, Harry, and Lawrence Wien. Leona kept everyone involved in the closing up until dawn, maniacally counting every towel and teacup in the hotel. I didn't see that happening with Bob Bass and John Aoki.

I took my first behind-the-scenes tour of the Plaza as an owner early in the summer of 1988 with Richard Wilhelm, our vice president and general manager. Although only in his mid-forties, Dick already had a great deal of hotel management experience, having worked at, among other places, the Waldorf-Astoria, the St. Regis, and Trump Castle. He understands that a great hotel is a living, breathing place that can be killed by complacency. When Ivana and I brought him from Atlantic City, where he'd set up an employee-training program that allowed workers to earn credits toward a degree in hotel administration from Michigan State, Dick was eager to roll up his sleeves and begin making changes. Fortunately, he shared our belief that at the Plaza we should forget about glitz and work toward restoring the hotel to its former grandeur.

"Before we start our tour," Dick said that day, with a twinkle in his eye, "I'm happy to inform you that you're going to be thoroughly appalled by some of what we're going to see."

I knew what he meant: that there were great opportunities for improvement along the way.

"Good," I said. "Let's start at the top."

The first thing I saw when I stepped out onto the Plaza roof was a magnificent sweeping view of one of the great crossroads of the world. The second thing I noticed was an old green paint shed that had been put up some thirty years before. Since 1947, when the original owners sold the hotel, the Plaza had been run by a succession of chain operators—Hilton, Sonesta, and Westin. All around the hotel there were signs of the mediocre management that's almost inevitable when large public corporations are involved, but this ugly rooftop structure was one of the most appalling. Standing there, I immediately started to visualize what could be one of the most spectacular residences in the world. "What an incredible waste," I said to Dick. "We could rip this down and make it over into the top floor of a beautiful duplex apartment that we could probably lease for a million dollars a year."

From there we walked down one flight to the nineteenth floor, which was taken up by 30,000 square feet of offices leased to the architectural firm of Lee Harris Pomeroy. Here again, the views of Central Park were spectacular, but the previous owners, panicking in the face of the bad times that had hit New York City in the late seventies, had seen fit to lease the entire floor for $10 a square foot, about the price of downtown warehouse space.

As I stood before a large photo of a Fifth Avenue building that was hanging in the hallway, I got an idea and knocked on the door of the boss, Lee Pomeroy. "Was this building your project?" I asked, pointing to the picture. He said it was, and he told me about some other things his firm was involved in. "I like your work," I said. "And I've got a proposition for you." What I wanted, I told him straight out, was to get back his space so that I could create luxury duplexes along the top floor of the Plaza. "I know you've got a good deal here," I said, "so how about this: If you agree to vacate by next March, you can be, along with Hardy Holzman Pfeiffer, the architect on the Plaza renovation, which could be the most exciting project you've ever done." His eyes lit up and we shook hands on a deal right there. Then I headed down to the next floor.

Things were rolling, and I was feeling great. Later, when I went into the archives and looked over the 1907 plans of architect Henry Hardenbergh, I discovered that his ideas had been strikingly similar to the ones I had in mind. That made me feel even better.

Westin had actually spent $89 million renovating the Plaza, but as I toured the building that day, I was stunned by how little of it showed. The marble staircases between floors were dull from wear and grime; many of the bedspreads in the Plaza's eight hundred rooms were stained beyond any hope of cleaning; and the bellmen's uniforms were frayed at the cuffs and were missing buttons.

One thing I found especially offensive, as I walked the hotel's spacious corridors, was that virtually all of the beautifully detailed moldings, which originally had been enhanced by real gold leaf, had simply been painted over with yellow or, in some cases, ugly brown paint. If that had been part of an organized campaign to cut costs, I might have been able to understand it. But for every dollar saved, thousands were being wasted. Everywhere I went in the hotel, I saw a precious commodity—floor area—being squandered. The entire eighth floor was serving as storage space, simply because, I guess, that's what always had been done. The biggest suite in the building—a duplex encompassing twenty rooms and a walk-in wine vault—was being used by the hotel's managing director as his private apartment. And at a time when the Plaza's catering staff was so busy it was turning people away, a great deal of space on the banquet-room level was taken by offices for the Plaza's personnel staff.

Something had to be done, and by the time the day was finished, I'd formulated a basic plan to clear eighty years' worth of garbage out of the basement, put in bright modern offices for the personnel people, and build new dining rooms that would allow us to increase revenues by several million dollars a year.

Ivana became president of the Plaza in June of 1988, moving over from Trump Castle. Barbara Res, the nononsense woman who had supervised the construction of Trump Tower, understood what I was after as well as anybody; that's why I put her in charge of the hotel's renovation.

I loved to pore over material in the archives. As I analyzed the old menus, souvenir books, and photographs, I felt as if I were trying to solve a mystery, which in a way I was—the mystery of exactly what the Plaza looked like in its glory days. And little by little the clues were adding up.

One day, while checking out something in an obscure corner of the Plaza's subbasement, I saw a beautiful brass clock, and then another and another, just gathering dust far back on some shelves. As it turned out, the Plaza used to have one of those clocks on the marble mantels of each of its 260 fireplaces. All the smaller clocks were connected to one central clock, which meant that all the timepieces in the hotel were precisely synchronized. It was a great old system. A few years before, though, some genius who was probably trying to impress the guy ahead of him in the corporate pecking order must have gotten the idea that the clocks were cheaper to store than to maintain, and so he relegated them to the basement. Ivana and I agreed that all 260 clocks should be cleaned, refitted with quartz works, and put back on the mantels as soon as possible.

Paging carefully one day through a marvelous 1907 copy of a magazine called *Architectural Record*, I saw an ad for a Brooklyn tile company that boasted it had installed the floor in the Plaza's Oak Room. At the present time, I knew, there was an old, wornout wall-to-wall carpet in the Oak Room. Ivana ordered one corner lifted to see what was underneath, and, sure enough, there was the beautiful mosaic floor that had been mentioned in the ad. The only problem was that it was marred in places by dirt and carpet glue. I went back to that old magazine, got the company's name, and looked it up. Not only was it still in business but the grandson of the man who'd originally laid the floor answered the phone. At our request, he came over to clean and restore the tile so that Oak Room patrons might once again see the fine mosaic work in all its glory.

Another idea we got from the archives was the restoration of the "champagne porch," which sits just above the front desk. Once a romantic little spot for sipping a drink while watching the traffic in the lobby below, the area was until recently boarded up with plywood painted to look like marble. Back in the forties, when air conditioning came in, the jewellike little space had been shut down because somebody decided it wasn't worth the extra cooling cost. I looked at it another way: The most practical thing I could do was enhance the Plaza as a work of art. The champagne porch, looking every bit as elegant as it did in the days of F. Scott Fitzgerald and John "Bet-a-Million" Gates, will make a triumphant return in 1992.

A lot of other ideas about how to restore the hotel came from employees who'd been there since the good old days. I remember walking through the ballroom one day with about twenty designers, consultants, architects, and others, all of whom were telling me that I should take down the curtains, move the doorways, and change everything around in ways that I frankly found mind-boggling. On an impulse, I grabbed one of the waiters and asked him how long he'd worked at the Plaza. "Thirty-seven years," he said. I then ushered him off to a quiet spot and began asking him questions. "Oh, Mr. Trump, we need the curtains because we have shows," he said. "But if you want to know what has to be changed, I'll tell you." In about five minutes, he and I had formulated a basic master plan for the renovation of the ballroom.

The key to improving the Plaza is that I move fast and decisively, unencumbered by any bureaucracy. I may not always make the right move—for instance, my announcement that Ivana would be paid one dollar a year and all the dresses she could buy got me in some trouble—but there is never any bureaucratic bullshit. I walk through the place, see things I don't like, and immediately work on getting them changed. When Ivana would call and say she wanted to spend $150,000 to redo each of the suites, she could get an answer—yes or no—in thirty seconds. It doesn't have to be a problem involving money, either. Not long after she took over at the Plaza, Ivana called me to say that she had asked the hotel maintenance people to imprint the sand in the lobby ashtrays with the Plaza logo, but the union leaders were giving her a hard time. I called the union and worked it out. If I'd been some corporate executive, we'd probably just now be having our third or fourth meeting on the issue.

Of course, I don't want to do everything at breakneck speed. I allowed my exterior architects, Hardy Holzman Pfeiffer Associates, as well as Lee Pomeroy's people, all the time they needed to develop a magnificent plan for bringing the Plaza back to its original state. The job before them wasn't easy. What I wanted entailed a great number of changes to the building, including adding fourteen new suites to the top and cutting windows through the magnificent green mansard roof. Meanwhile, whatever they did would have to please not just me but the city's Landmarks Preservation Commission, as well as the critics and the people of New York. I'm happy to say they came through like champions with the most sensitive and historically accurate renovation I'd ever seen. In addition to removing the storage structure on the roof, their plan called for the creation of a stunning interior light-well over the Palm Court, the restoration of the Fifth Avenue entrance lobby, the rebirth of the Rose Room, the addition of turn-of-the-century decorative awnings, and numerous other improvements inside and out.

Not only did the Landmarks Commission approve the proposal, but Paul Goldberger, *The New York Times* critic, reviewed the renovation plan and gave it unqualified raves. "There is no building New Yorkers feel as possessive about as the Plaza," Goldberger started out. He then went on to praise the plan virtually point by point and acknowledged that the hotel wasn't a museum piece but a constantly evolving environment.

In September 1988 I took a full page in *The New York Times*. Under the headline WHY I BOUGHT THE PLAZA I wrote:

> I haven't purchased a building, I have purchased a masterpiece—the Mona Lisa.
>
> For the first time in my life, I have knowingly made a deal which was not economic—for I can never justify the price I paid, no matter how successful the Plaza becomes. What I have done, however, is to give to New York City the opportunity to have a hotel which transcends all others. The Plaza will transcend all others! I am committed to making the Plaza New York's single greatest hotel, perhaps the greatest hotel in the world.

As soon as I had purchased the Plaza I realized that the St. Moritz didn't fit into my current plans. I'd had a great run with the place, buying it for $71 million in 1985, and managing it to a gross operating profit averaging $11.5 million every year since. But I didn't need to compete with myself by owning another large hotel, also in need of renovation, just one block west of the Plaza on Central Park South. I wanted a neat, clean, quick deal for the St. Moritz so that I could keep my attention focused on the Plaza. But because the St. Moritz was so successful and had such a prime location, I didn't see why I should make a financial sacrifice just to make a sale.

My solution to this dilemma was to call Alan Bond, a wealthy Australian investor. I first met Alan a few years ago, when he was supporting an Australian syndicate in the America's Cup yacht races and I was backing an American sailing team that was determined to get the prize back. He impressed me then as one of the world's great characters, a guy who shot from the hip and took his chances as they came. A few years later, I watched in amazement as he got caught up in a major art auction and wound up paying a record $53.9 million for van Gogh's *Irises*. Alan, I realized at that point, doesn't mess around.

When I phoned him, he was openly interested in the St. Moritz from the start. And when he came to see me in my office later, he was there only about twenty minutes before we'd signed a letter of agreement saying that he'd bought the hotel for $180 million, giving me a profit of $110 million not including its operating profit. The only negotiating we did came when Alan offered me *Irises* as partial payment. I told him I just couldn't accept the painting. ''What would I do with it?'' I asked him.

To be frank, I don't see how he can run the St. Moritz profitably at the price he paid. In the interim Alan has encountered financial problems. But he was happy when he left and, naturally, so was I. I predict that Alan will make a great comeback.

A lot of the profit I made on the St. Moritz has been poured back into the Plaza. I won't be satisfied until all the gold leaf glitters, every inch of marble sparkles, and each bronze handrail shines.

Even if I wanted to be cavalier about the hotel, the public wouldn't let me. I'm still amazed by the uproar I caused when I announced that I was closing Trader Vic's. To me, it was little more than a bar and restaurant off the lobby specializing in fake Polynesian cuisine and exotic drinks loaded with tiny plastic swords and paper umbrellas. I envisioned turning the space into a health club, or perhaps a nineties version of Le Club, the exclusive haunt where I'd spent many evenings just after I moved to Manhattan. When I said Trader Vic's had gotten tacky, however, a lot of people objected to my criticizing a part of my own hotel. How dare I denigrate the place where they'd gone after their senior prom, they said. In response to my announcement, so many people poured in for a sentimental drink and one last pu-pu platter that I decided to keep the place open for the time being.

Ultimately, though, the Plaza will be remembered as the finest hotel not only in New York City but in the world.

That's already happening. Not long ago, the *Condé*

Nast Traveler ran a major story in which they asked twenty-five of the world's leading hoteliers where they would choose to stay while traveling. The Plaza was the only New York hotel on the list compiled by those discriminating people—people, as the magazine said, "sensitive to the smallest imperfection." I'd like to share with you what James Daley, the owner of the sumptuous Copley Plaza Hotel in Boston, said about the Plaza in that article:

> We had champagne waiting on our arrival. Bathrobes, hair dryers, and Chanel perfume were in the room. The entire first floor was being finished, and the function rooms and the ballroom were lovely, done in red. Room service was fast, and the staff was pleasant. We needed tickets to a play at the last minute, and the concierge got them for us. It was all done in a grand style.
>
> Donald stopped by our table while we were having dinner in the Oak Room. The food was excellent.

Ivana, Dick Wilhelm, and the entire staff have done a fantastic job. The hotel has truly been turned around. The final word on the Plaza has yet to be written, but I do know that I've taken a world-famous one-of-a-kind institution and enhanced its value. As a businessman and a lover of fine buildings, I can live with that for now.

SEVEN

FLYING HIGH
The Shuttle Story

AT five o'clock on May 24, 1989, a loud cheer went up in my suite of offices. Thanks to a court ruling in my favor, the Eastern Shuttle would at last become the Trump Shuttle and take to the skies.

The news from the court ended one of the longest, toughest battles I'd ever waged. But while everyone else was celebrating our entrance into a new business, I had a feeling of déjà vu. The Eastern Shuttle reminded me very much of the Plaza Hotel. Both were great American institutions that had deteriorated badly in terms of their image and the service they provided. And now both were mine, to preserve and improve as best I could, while the world watched.

The shuttle deal had begun a few years earlier with

a phone call I received from Frank Lorenzo. Frank, who had taken over Eastern Airlines not long before, asked if he might drop by my office to discuss an idea he was working on. Since I'd always been intrigued by the airline business, and since there's never any harm in talking, I said sure, and we made an appointment for the next day.

At that time I didn't know Frank personally, but I was well aware of his reputation as the CEO of Texas Air Corporation. Frank was known as a tough, cold takeover artist, a guy who bought troubled airlines like Continental, People Express, and New York Air, and then turned them into low-cost operations, usually by breaking the unions, slashing salaries, and lopping off unprofitable operations. He always had very little to say to the press—which meant that the union leaders, his avowed enemies, wound up shaping his public image. They depicted him, with their quotes and stories, as an evil, Darth Vader-type character, an executive who was, to say the least, no friend of the working man.

When he came up to my office, Frank didn't strike me as an ogre. I did notice, however, that he dispensed with all small talk and got quickly to the point—a plan to create a subsidiary of Texas Air that would buy the shuttle from Eastern. Would I be interested, he asked, in becoming an investor, along with him and a few others, in this proposed shuttle spin-off?

In some respects it was an intriguing idea. Eastern's

New York–Washington and New York–Boston runs had been profitable practically from the day they were introduced in the early sixties. The shuttle, more than just a means of transportation, was now a way of life for the influential people who traveled the so-called power corridor in the Northeast. On top of that, Eastern had the best locations at the airports in each of the three shuttle cities, as well as a tradition of flights every hour on the hour, a seemingly simple bit of scheduling that in fact gave the airline a huge advantage over the competition.

Normally, no executive in his right mind would sell off such a crown jewel. And Frank was very much in control of his faculties. So what was this all about?

Actually, the situation was easy to understand. Eastern was a company in dire financial straits. To keep the once-proud airline going, Frank desperately needed the cash that the sale of the shuttle would bring.

As I sat listening to Frank, I couldn't help but be impressed by some of his qualities. He had the lean, almost gaunt, look of a guy who had tremendous mental and physical endurance—the result, I learned later, of his long-distance jogging. Judging by the plan he outlined, I believed he was also a first-class dealmaker. But while his idea was interesting, it wasn't for me.

What Frank was looking for was basically a backer for an operation that he would run. I don't like putting up large amounts of money and then having someone else decide how a project will be handled.

"There's no kick in it for me unless I can go out, find the best people, and then manage the company," I told Frank. "But," I added, "if the Eastern Shuttle ever comes on the market, I'd love to buy it."

Although I meant what I said, I didn't really think I'd get a chance at the shuttle, a world-class asset, again.

Many months later, however, at a time when thoughts of Eastern were far from my mind, I got a call from Frank, asking if I was still interested. By then he had dropped his plan to buy the operation himself through a subsidiary. Now he was talking about a deal that offered exactly what I wanted—a chance to acquire and operate that small gem of an airline on my own.

"Yes," I said, "I'm definitely interested." We arranged to meet for breakfast the next morning.

Without letting myself get too excited, I felt I had a strong shot at getting the shuttle. Frank, I knew, had to do something about Eastern Airlines, and quickly. The company had been in bad shape when he took over from Frank Borman, the former astronaut, in 1986. Now, not only was Eastern continuing to hemorrhage money, but it seemed on the verge of a civil war. A huge number of pilots had quit in the course of the last year, other workers were passing around pictures of Frank with a target drawn over his face, and there were even reports of physical violence. At one point, Alfred Kahn, the former chairman of the

Civil Aeronautics Board, said that Frank and Charles Bryan, the head of the machinists union, were like "two scorpions in a bottle. The hatred is so great," he noted, "that they seem prepared to ruin the airline."

Through it all, Frank just kept quiet and took the heat. In life, most people are big talk and no action. Frank is that rare person who is all action and no talk. I'm not saying that's a good thing, because some talk perhaps could have eased the tension with the unions and prevented the continuing decline of Eastern. But no amount of pressure could make Frank reveal what he might do if the machinists struck, how he felt about the possibility of taking Eastern into bankruptcy, or any of the other issues then threatening the airline's very existence.

The funny thing is, I found Frank, man-to-man, to be a very different guy from the reclusive, evil maniac you read about in the business press. I met with him numerous times over the next couple of months, always in the Edwardian Room of the Plaza Hotel, and invariably found him relaxed, charming, and compassionate, despite his feelings about the union leaders. Frank is also a devoted family man who cares very deeply about his wife, Sharon, and their children.

As a dealmaker, though, Frank turned out to be, as expected, quite tough. In the shuttle he had an extremely valuable asset under his control and from the start of the negotiations it was clear he knew it.

Frank's asking price for the shuttle and seventeen

Boeing 727s was $425 million. I thought I could get it for less and made a counteroffer of $325 million.

I kept stressing to Frank that by selling to me, not only would he get a buyer who could secure financing with no problem, but, perhaps just as important, he would keep a potentially profitable operation away from his competitors. "In all fairness, you might get more from American or United," I said to Frank. "But why make the competition stronger?" Ultimately he agreed, and we settled on a price of $365 million and signed contracts.

We were both pleased with the deal we'd made, but at the press conference we called to announce the sale, I saw that Frank was either unable or unwilling to communicate his good feelings to the public. As soon as the reporters began asking questions, Frank got tense and combative, and he came off looking like the villain everyone assumed he was. Frank flew off the handle at the very first question, in fact, and—something that I had never seen before—the reporter actually wanted to leave the room, he was so offended by Frank's attitude.

Unfortunately, my initial delight in the shuttle deal didn't last long. A few days after we'd signed our agreement, Eastern's three unions filed a lawsuit attempting to block the sale.

The pilots, machinists, and flight attendants believed, rightly or wrongly, that the sale of Eastern's crown jewel could make it impossible for the company to remain a force in the airline business. They felt this was the first step in the dismantling of Eastern Airlines, a process that could lead to the loss of their jobs or, at the very least, deep pay cuts.

Whether or not that was actually Frank's intention, no one knew. The unions, however, were willing to believe anything bad about Frank—and eager to do anything that might screw up his plans.

Eastern's attorneys were very worried about winning the case, but not because they had doubts about our legal position. What concerned them was that our case was being heard in federal court by Barrington Parker, a judge who had previously ruled against Eastern in a case the company thought it would win. Eastern's people believed, perhaps with some justification, that Judge Parker felt a strong animosity toward them and their controversial leader.

When we met to discuss our strategy in the case, I told Eastern's lawyers that I wanted to testify. Their immediate reaction was to veto the idea. It was too risky, they said—too bold, such things just weren't done, and so on. They had a million reasons why I should stay on the sidelines.

I, on the other hand, thought it would help our case, because the image of Donald Trump, in the minds of many, is that of a flamethrower, a tyrant, a businessman who goes around destroying his competition. If I could take the stand, I felt, I could show that that image, at least in many respects, is false.

"If the judge sees I'm a decent guy and not the wild man portrayed in the media," I told the Eastern people, "it can only help our case. And besides," I added, "you feel you're fighting a totally uphill battle anyway, so what do you have to lose?"

Finally, one really sharp lawyer from the Eastern team, David Boies of Cravath Swaine & Moore, had the guts to say he agreed with me. It was Boies's recommendation that persuaded Eastern to allow me to testify.

In the end, my testimony before Judge Parker went very well. While I was on the stand, I was able to make the points that Eastern Airlines was in tremendous trouble and that the employees were in a very precarious position. I also noted that if the shuttle deal was not made and Eastern did not receive my $365 million, everyone at the airline could soon be out of work. Finally, I pointed out that the asset was eroding and soon would be worth far less than the price I was willing to pay.

As I spoke, I could sense that all of these arguments had a great impact on the judge, who I found to be a wonderful guy.

We won the lawsuit, and with legal distractions behind me—or so I thought—I plunged back into the process of getting the Trump Shuttle off the ground. By this time I had hired a team, including executives who had helped start the Pan Am Shuttle. They, in turn, had put together a staff that was working on getting all the necessary FAA approvals and licenses, as well as hiring pilots and other employees, putting together a marketing plan, and bringing in designers to refurbish the 727s I was getting from Eastern. It was a huge undertaking, but everyone's adrenaline was flowing, and morale in my newly created shuttle division couldn't have been higher.

Then one day, in the midst of all our preparations, we got word that the unions had appealed Judge Parker's decision.

In a way, this wasn't surprising. All the unions cared about at that point was destroying Frank Lorenzo. It was almost as if he were the devil and had to be defeated at all costs.

If you got past the emotions, however, what the unions were doing was tremendously self-destructive. After all, here I was, a new player who wanted to forge an alliance with labor as I launched the Trump Shuttle. Now, by pursuing an appeal, the very people who would benefit from my getting the shuttle were delaying, and possibly ruining, my deal.

The appeal process would take a long time, and while their case was pending, I couldn't close. If I gave a check for $365 million to Eastern, which was headed for bankruptcy, and the unions won, I could be forced to give back the shuttle even though Eastern might not have the money to refund to me. Although

I was eager to get the shuttle going and was confident of victory, I couldn't risk $365 million under those circumstances.

Another thing that worried me was that while the appeal process dragged on, I'd have to continue working very hard to get all my approvals in order, and hire hundreds of employees in anticipation of taking over the shuttle quickly. In other words, great amounts of time, energy, and money were being spent in preparation for an asset that in the end might never arrive. Threatening my position even further was Eastern's possible bankruptcy. That could take the shuttle out of my control and put its fate in the hands of a judge whose concern would be to see if anyone wanted to top my bid and take the asset away.

On March 4, 1989, the machinists struck the airline and—to the surprise, I think, of Frank Lorenzo—the pilots and flight attendants honored the picket lines. What that meant in a nutshell was that Eastern could fly only a tiny percentage of its routes. If the planes couldn't fly, there'd be no revenue. And if there was no revenue, bankruptcy couldn't be far off.

With the situation worsening daily, I called Frank Lorenzo and spoke bluntly of my concerns.

"Look, I know where Eastern is going," I said, "and I'm aware that you may have to file for bankruptcy. That's your business. But I deserve some protection."

More than anything, I wanted to avoid being used

as a stalking horse who would endorse the shuttle as a good deal but in the end not get it because the bankruptcy court and its board of creditors awarded it to a higher bidder. It seems that when I want to buy something, a lot of people come out of the woodwork waving money. That's what happened with Merv Griffin and the Resorts International deal. These people operate on the theory that if I've bid on something, it must be worth considerably more than what I'm offering.

To protect myself in case the shuttle wound up in bankruptcy court, I asked Frank to amend our agreement. The clause I wanted said that a substantial fee would be paid to me by Eastern if for any reason the shuttle went to someone else. We fought long and hard on this point. But in the end Frank agreed that a fee of $8 million would go to me if the shuttle wound up with another buyer.

That was one of my better moves because it allowed me the security of knowing I could invest a large amount of money in the shuttle and still walk away with a slight profit if I didn't get what I was after. But what was even more significant than the money was the position that agreement put me in. Because I could continue working full speed ahead, I could close a deal for the shuttle six months before anyone else—anyone, that is, except an already established airline. In the eyes of the bankruptcy court, being able to move with that kind of speed would give me a great advantage.

It's a good thing I was prepared for a worst-case scenario, because things at Eastern certainly weren't getting any better. The airline had managed to keep the shuttle flying after the strike, but market share was diminishing steadily. Passengers didn't want to cross picket lines, especially to fly on an airline whose regular mechanics weren't coming to work. Even an attempt to promote the shuttle by charging lower fares had no lasting effect on load levels. The asset was deteriorating before my eyes.

I called Frank Lorenzo and asked, once again, to renegotiate our deal.

He wasn't exactly happy to hear from me, but with market share down from 56 to 17 percent, he probably wasn't surprised, either.

"Frank," I said, "the value of what I bought from you is disintegrating. Pan Am is picking up customers not because they're good, but just because they're there."

What I asked him to do, ultimately, was to include an additional five 727s in our $365 million deal as compensation for the diminished value of the shuttle. We argued bitterly over this point, but finally Frank agreed to give me the planes. That was a minor victory. It increased the value of my deal and allowed me to refurbish my fleet without taking any needed planes out of service.

I was actually starting to feel optimistic again about the shuttle at this point because I'd made something good out of a very bad situation. But if the story of this deal proves anything, it is the value of perseverance in the face of adversity.

On March 9, the other shoe finally dropped when Eastern filed for bankruptcy. When that happened, control of the company passed from Frank Lorenzo to the bankruptcy court and board of creditors, and, one by one, people who wanted to take over the airline began emerging.

One of the first was Peter Ueberroth, who had just resigned as baseball commissioner.

Peter is a wonderful and talented guy whose idea was to put together a coalition of investors and unions. I never understood how he expected the company to be profitable the way he was restructuring it, nor am I sure to this day if it included the purchase of the shuttle. In the end, it really doesn't matter, because Ueberroth's deal fell through when the unions insisted that Frank Lorenzo had to be replaced immediately by a caretaker figure before any deal could be struck.

Around this time the name of Carl Icahn also surfaced as a possible buyer for Eastern. Carl, a great business mind, had once forged an alliance with the unions and gained control of TWA at a time when Frank Lorenzo was very interested in acquiring that airline. It would have been interesting, to say the least, to see those two in action. But Icahn must not have liked what he found out about Eastern because the deal never got past the talking stage.

The real shocker was when a relatively little-known company called America West Airlines arrived on the scene from Phoenix, Arizona.

America West was intent on getting the shuttle, and it approached the bankruptcy court and the board of Eastern creditors that had been set up to handle such matters with a complex bid that was, under any of the various options they proposed, at least $100 million higher than mine. I remember getting the news and then walking into my brother's office and saying, "Well, our deal is dead."

I didn't know much about America West at that time, but as pessimistic as I was, I did some research on the company. What I found was that it was one of the few new start-up airlines that had been able to survive, and it was highly thought of on Wall Street. It had a very aggressive management and a very good reputation for passenger service. The problem was that in the two years prior to its bid it had experienced some financial difficulties. Its aggressiveness had caused a certain overextension in terms of financing, and it had lost money. However, in the current year it was doing very well and was in fact showing a profit.

Since it seemed to be such a sharp outfit, I was truly surprised at how much higher its bid was than mine. But I figured that, given the company's reputation, it must have its financing. Usually when a company bids on an asset, especially in a situation where its offer becomes front-page news in *The Wall Street Journal* and many other papers, it has its money lined up in advance and is not going in with a deal that can't be consummated.

Though the situation looked bad, I didn't feel defeated. Instead, I called in Harvey Freeman, a top executive of mine who had been instrumental in hammering out our agreement with Frank Lorenzo.

"Now," I said to Harvey, "the war begins."

The first thing Harvey and I did was dig deeper into my America West research. Once we did, I started to see flaws that might be exploited. The company was highly leveraged, and despite the fact that it had made a small profit that year and was obviously heading in the right direction, its balance sheet was not at all strong.

I then told Harvey, Robert, and all my top people that I wanted the world to know about the shaky state of America West. It wouldn't be hard getting the word out, I knew. The media were all over the Eastern story.

A couple of days later, I found myself speaking with a writer from *The Wall Street Journal*, which from the start had covered the entire Eastern Airlines affair very extensively. I described to the reporter at length what I'd found out about the company, then concluded by saying, "In my opinion, if America West does this transaction and pays the ridiculous price that it's offering, it will quickly become the next People

Express.'' In other words, I was saying that their offer was so excessive that it would lead them quickly into bankruptcy.

The next day the *Journal* ran a story in the right-hand column on the front page—the most prestigious space in the paper—based largely on my interview. The headline read AMERICA WEST'S BID FOR EASTERN SHUTTLE MAY POSE BIG RISKS; RIVAL BIDDER TRUMP DOUBTS ITS FINANCIAL RESOURCES; PRIOR EXPANSION BACKFIRED.

The story started like this: ''Donald Trump can barely hide his contempt for America West Airlines, a carrier he claims he never heard of before it topped his offer for the Eastern Shuttle with a $415 million bid.''

Then it continued with a quote from me: ''You just have to look at their balance sheet to see that this is not a company in a position to overpay for the shuttle. This is not IBM. If I were a bank I wouldn't loan them money for anything.''

From there the story went on to explain, in the writer's words, the difficulties America West was having with financing.

The Wall Street Journal—right or wrong—has a lot of power, and that front-page story illustrated it vividly. Consider that the judge had set a deadline for financing and that America West was very close to getting its financing on the morning the article appeared. In less than twenty-four hours, America West was devastated. As a result of that one *Journal* story, shock waves went through all of Wall Street and the entire financial and airline communities, and America West lost its credibility. At the last moment, despite the airline's repeated announcements that it would have no trouble getting the money to back its bid, America West announced that it had to withdraw its offer for lack of financing.

The judge then ruled that the shuttle was mine.

The defeat of America West not only made me feel great, it made me very popular with certain banks. What had been perceived as a solid business transaction just a couple of weeks before now looked like one of the great deals of the decade. Suddenly everyone was running to loan me money to buy this wonderful asset, and though I already had my financing, from Citibank, I was inundated with calls from other institutions wanting to know if they could take a piece of the financing, or lead it, and promising me all kinds of better deals. In retrospect, considering the market conditions that have affected the shuttle, it now appears they shouldn't have been making those offers.

I just shook my head and smiled. Success, so often, is just a matter of perception. This was the same deal I'd had for months. But because another company had come in, bid substantially more, and then dropped out, I was suddenly seen as a bigger winner than before.

The shuttle deal also proved the value of being a

poker player. When America West came along, everyone wanted me to raise my bid by as much as $100 million to ensure that I'd get the shuttle. I knew, though, that I wasn't going to raise my bid by even one cent. I wanted to stand pat and take my chances. If someone was willing to spend hundreds of millions more than I was, then I would let him have what he wanted and wish him good luck.

It was a tense experience; under slightly different circumstances the deal could have gone a lot more smoothly. But when I look back on the situation, I think of a friend of mine, a very good and talented politician who was running for office unopposed, or so he thought. At the last moment a very strong challenger announced he was running for the same spot. Initially my friend was devastated. From one day to the next he had gone from having an easy campaign to facing the prospect of much hard work followed by possible defeat. But he didn't give up. Instead, he ran a great campaign and ended up beating the hell out of his opponent. I'll never forget his coming to me afterward and telling me that the challenge was the best thing that ever happened to him—it transformed a nonevent into a major political victory. Because he had to fight his way into office, the victory was much sweeter.

I know what he meant. In retrospect, I'm glad America West came along. They wound up giving me—and the Trump Shuttle—a tremendous boost.

It should be noted that one of the people most helpful to the labor cause after the nonunion America West arrived on the scene was New York State governor Mario Cuomo. Through his brilliant economic development adviser, Vincent Tese, the chairman of the New York State Urban Development Corporation, Cuomo let it be known that he was tired of seeing the Eastern unions pushed around. He had little compassion for a nonunion carrier like America West, which came in from Phoenix to exploit an already sad situation. By exerting his influence, Governor Cuomo did a truly great service for the union employees of the Trump Shuttle, not only in preserving jobs but in helping them gain a great moral victory.

When I took over the shuttle from Eastern, it had only about 17 percent of the market. Today the Trump Shuttle is running beautifully, with impeccably maintained aircraft that look great on the ground or in the air. As I write this, our market share has grown to about 50 percent. That sounds good, but frankly it's disappointing to me because we have a far better operation—terminals, planes, service—than Pan Am.

I was a little worried when I took over the shuttle because I was aware that Eastern was known for its animosity toward passengers and its bad service. I had assumed that this attitude was ingrained in the people who worked for Eastern.

Was I ever wrong.

The level of employee spirit and of service to the

passengers of the new Trump Shuttle has been far higher than it would have been if I'd gone out and hired all new workers. The Eastern employees had been stifled for years. When they were released, there was a tremendous burst of energy. They wanted to prove that they could do the job. They wanted to show the public and the world that everybody had been wrong about them. And, boy, have they been able to show it.

Perhaps the most spectacular example of the kind of people I have working on my planes is Captain Bob Smith.

It was on a rainy summer afternoon a few months after I bought the shuttle that I first heard of this extraordinary pilot. I was in the middle of a routine phone conversation trying to convince McDonald's to lease a piece of land I owned in Brooklyn for a hamburger stand. I was negotiating with the McDonald's representatives, telling them my site was the greatest site in the history of fast food or whatever, when one of my executives came into my office and said that he had to speak with me immediately.

I put McDonald's on hold.

"I've got good news and bad news," this executive said, matter-of-factly. "The good news is that we have a master pilot on the plane."

"Huh?" I said to him. "What plane are you talking about?"

"That's the bad news," he said. "I'm talking about

the plane that's circling Logan Airport in Boston because one wheel won't come down.''

The first thing I did was to turn on the TV. And there, live on CNN, was my plane coming in for a landing. The approach seemed to go on forever, but finally Captain Smith touched that 727 down perfectly.

I couldn't believe things had gone as smoothly as it looked, but a few minutes later the passengers started appearing on camera and saying it had been like a regular landing. They hadn't felt a thing. In fact, I later checked the records and virtually all of them who were making return trips to New York came back on the Trump Shuttle.

''I've got to go up and congratulate that pilot,'' I said.

By that time, various members of my staff had gathered around the TV to watch the landing. They all looked at me as if I were crazy.

''It'll just make for a day of bad press about the Trump Shuttle, more negative stuff,'' one of them said, speaking for the group. ''Let it pass.''

It was a classic management problem: to go or not to go. But with all due respect to those fine people, they were making the wrong decision.

''I know how airlines traditionally treat these matters,'' I said. ''But there's nothing negative about this. Negative is a catastrophe. What we've got here is an excellent pilot showing talent and grace under pressure—a hero.''

I immediately went up to Boston on the next shuttle flight to publicly congratulate Bob Smith and the entire crew. The media attention we received as a result of my visit was overwhelmingly positive. The next day, the Trump Shuttle numbers were substantially up.

For all the progress, however, the situation with the shuttle remains complicated. Business travel in the Northeast is down overall, and costs are up more than we planned for. I even told a *Wall Street Journal* reporter that I would sell if I got the right price.

Gradually I've come to realize—as I have with the Plaza—that restoring a great asset is not enough to cover expenses when you're paying off a large acquisition debt. I made a tactical mistake in saying publicly that I might sell the shuttle, because people's confidence in the airline is bound to be shaken if I seem to be pulling out. The shuttle is now profitable. Frankly, I'm glad I saved it. I'm proud of the way it's been improved. It is now the best.

I *had* read a lot about him during the last several years, and I found his fall from grace absolutely fascinating.

That's why, when Norma came in and told me that someone was calling from England regarding the sale of Khashoggi's famous yacht, I dropped whatever I was doing and reached for the phone.

I've never been much of a boat person. And because of that, I frankly didn't know what the broker, an Englishman named Jonathan Beckett, was talking about when he mentioned words like "tenders," "bilges," and "dinghies." I couldn't even say if the price Beckett was asking for the yacht—$50 million —was realistic, though I suspected I could get it cheaper. All I knew for sure was that I wanted that vessel.

Usually, when I do a deal, it fits into some larger plan. I buy a hotel on the Boardwalk in Atlantic City because I need the rooms for my casino customers, or I invest in a department store chain, like Alexander's, because the company owns some very desirable real estate. But my purchase of that yacht was something else entirely. It was a deal done strictly for the sake of dealing: art for art's sake. In a way, it reminded me of when I bought Mar-a-Lago, my house in Palm Beach. I didn't *need* a 118-room house in Florida, and I didn't need this 282-foot boat, either. I just saw an opportunity to acquire something at a fantastic price, and I seized the moment.

The yacht had been an important tool of Khashoggi's trade—I knew that much as I listened to Jonathan Beckett's sales pitch on the phone that day. With its huge kitchens and wine cellar and its fuel tanks big enough to take it around the world without stopping, the *Nabila*, as it was then known, was the ultimate party boat. It came complete, Jonathan said, with a private deck for sunbathing, massage and steam rooms, and a mind-boggling master bedroom with a tortoiseshell ceiling and a bed big enough for six people. The bathroom just off the master's quarters had a shower stall carved out of solid onyx. One room was full of pinball machines and video games. There was also a disco that had a state-of-the-art laser lighting system, a machine that sent smoke swirling around the dance floor, and a paneled ceiling in which pictures of Khashoggi, his guests, and his family flashed on and off in time to the music.

"It's the ultimate in opulence," Jon Beckett said.

I agreed that it sounded incredible. But in my opinion the Khashoggi touches were more than a little too much. After all, there were secret doors allowing guests to slip in and out of one another's rooms discreetly and two-way mirrors for voyeurs. I have since learned that Khashoggi, at the height of his success, rented an entire floor of a hotel in Monte Carlo, where the beautiful women who came to his parties would stay. I have no interest in making moral judgments about people, so I can't say I was shocked to learn about the wild parties that took place on board the *Nabila*—which Khashoggi had named, by the way, for his daughter. I don't think anything could shock me anymore.

Not that wild behavior is all that common among the rich and famous. Most successful people I know are, on the contrary, so wrapped up in their work that they never let their hair down. Unless you like to talk about real estate deals or the stock market, you'll probably find their company boring.

I don't include Khashoggi in that group.

Although I wasn't particularly happy to see Khashoggi being forced to sell his magnificent yacht, I can honestly say I didn't mind being the beneficiary.

Jonathan Beckett has since told me that negotiations for a large yacht sometimes take two or three years to complete. The deal for Khashoggi's boat, however, went swiftly and relatively smoothly. There was no reason why it shouldn't. I was an interested buyer, and the seller was even more eager than I was.

Khashoggi's life was such a mess at that point that he no longer owned the *Nabila*. It had passed into the hands of the sultan of Brunei, who took it in settlement of a $50 million loan. From my point of view that made little difference. Either way, I was still dealing with someone who wanted to unload the yacht as quickly as possible.

About twenty minutes into the first phone conversation I ever had about the yacht I offered to buy it for $15 million. Beckett, who had called me cold to discuss the opportunity, must have been shocked. In the first place, he knew that I had seen the boat only once, when I happened to be in Monte Carlo and caught a glimpse of it at the pier. I can—and often do—make major decisions right on the spot, and that sometimes blows people away. One of my greatest advantages is that I am an individual, not a corporation, and I don't have to go back to headquarters and deal with a bureaucracy.

Another reason Beckett probably couldn't believe what he was hearing was that it was such a lowball offer. Considering that the yacht had probably cost $85 million to build in the early eighties, and that to construct an identical boat would cost between $150 million and $200 million at the time, I knew that my price was unrealistic and that I'd have to pay more if I really wanted the boat. But I wanted to see right away if the *Nabila* was going to be the bargain I thought it might be. If Beckett rejected my offer and the conversation stopped right there, I'd know I wasn't going to get a great price, and that would probably be the beginning and the end of my fascination with boating. Jonathan's response, though, was that he would arrange to fly in from London so that we could talk further. I took that as a sign that my ridiculously low offer might not be so ridiculous after all.

Sometimes the most glamorous and highly publicized deals are no more complicated, basically, than what happens every day on any used-car lot. Certainly this negotiation was anything but complex. When Beckett walked into my office a few days later, he was asking $32 million for the vessel. I countered with $28 million, figuring we'd settle eventually on $30 million—which we did, after about thirty minutes of conversation.

The next day, after the story popped up in the newspapers, dozens of people called Jonathan Beckett's firm, Nigel Burgess, offering to beat my offer by several million dollars. I had warned Jon that that was going to happen, and so neither of us was surprised when people who hadn't been heard from before were suddenly trying to top my bid. I don't think Jon even took their phone calls.

There was, however, one unexpected development after we came to an agreement on price. I got a call from a representative of the sultan of Brunei, who said that Khashoggi was worried that his daughter's name would be used on the boat. Of course, I had no intention of continuing to call the yacht the *Nabila*. But my first reaction was not to give away anything without getting something in return.

"I'll think about it," I said. And I did—until the intermediary called back a few days later to say that the sultan, out of respect for Khashoggi, was prepared to knock $1 million off the purchase price if I agreed to change the name of the boat. I said that would be fine, and the final purchase price became $29 million.

Now I faced the question of what I was going to do with the boat.

As much as I loved it as a work of art, I knew that it would never become part of my personal life-style. I might enjoy cruising around the world as I wandered through the yacht's five decks and hundred-odd rooms—who knows? Realistically speaking, I knew I'd never try doing that. It makes me nervous to relax.

Instead I saw a great opportunity to use the *Trump Princess* for business purposes. I could give parties in New York for visiting dignitaries, and I could invite the media on board whenever I had a big new project to announce. But where the yacht would fit best, I sensed, was in Atlantic City. Not only was I building a magnificent new marina at Trump Castle, but the yacht seemed made to order for a town where the high rollers gravitate toward opulence and luxury.

The plan I envisioned was to make the *Trump Princess* a kind of floating suite for high rollers. Only the most important customers of the Trump Castle, the Trump Plaza, and eventually the Taj Mahal would be granted the privilege of staying on board and having my full crew at their disposal at absolutely no cost. This, I knew, played right into the psychology of the high roller. These are a very diverse bunch of people, but they all live life to the hilt. They expect the best, and they do not suffer fools, or foolish situations, gladly. The *Trump Princess*, I knew, would be made to order for people who can't be pampered enough.

Before I got too far along with my plans, though, I had to close on the yacht—something that proved far more difficult than negotiating the basic deal. One problem was that there were various components of the boat scattered throughout the Mediterranean. One of the "tenders"—a launch, I had just learned, which takes passengers back and forth between the boat and the dock—was in Antibes. Two others were in Monte Carlo. The yacht itself, meanwhile, was in San Remo, Italy. There was no way that I could take time away from my other businesses to fly over there and scout around and inspect everything. So, as eager as I was to finally step aboard the *Trump Princess*, I asked Jeff Walker if he would take care of the closing.

Jeff, a friend since we both attended New York Military Academy, is a vice president in charge of special projects for the Trump Organization. I call Jeff "the Eye" because he has a great aesthetic sense and also because, like me, he isn't dazzled by beauty; when he looks at something that everyone else is bowled over by, he homes in on the same small imperfections that I myself never fail to see. Besides that, Jeff grew up around the docks, and he knows boats.

Unfortunately, having Jeff representing me didn't mean I'd have a quick closing. Every day all of the lawyers and advisers for both sides would get on the yacht and motor off to a point at least twelve miles from the Italian coast so the deal could be consummated in international waters and nobody would have to pay taxes. And every evening the *Trump Princess* would come back to San Remo without anyone's having signed the sales agreement.

It wasn't that either side was being inflexible; the problem was that there was a huge inventory list to go over, and we had to make sure all of the silver, handmade linens, and valuable crystal that I'd negotiated to have included in the purchase price was in fact on board. After days of sailing around and checking, it turned out that very little was missing. Khashoggi had left behind many extremely valuable items made of gold, silver, and porcelain. Oddly enough, several pinball machines that couldn't have been worth more than a few hundred dollars were missing.

Once we'd finally closed on the deal, I flew to Italy to see the boat at last. Walking through the *Trump Princess* the first time, I was thrilled—and honestly surprised. I had expected something fabulous, but this was even better than I had imagined. It was obvious that Khashoggi had spared no expense. He had obtained the finest leathers, suedes, and other fabrics. The workmanship on the curved door to each stateroom was absolutely stunning. The woodwork throughout the boat, in fact, was like nothing I'd ever seen. If you opened a closet and pulled out a drawer, you found that the inside of the drawer had the same beautifully lacquered finish as the outside of the closet. And there were high-tech touches everywhere. A button on the night table next to the master bed automatically opened a drawer that contained more buttons for turning on the television and air conditioning and lowering the movie screen.

At the same time, there were signs that the yacht had been used hard. For example, there were dozens of little indentations in the ceiling where champagne corks had bounced off it and left their mark. Then there were the stains on the carpet and the worn spots on some sofas. Those things might not have bothered most people, but they set off alarm bells in me.

"I want this boat to look perfect," I said to Jeff Walker, who accompanied me as I strolled the decks. "Anything that's worn I want replaced. Anything that's soiled I want deep-cleaned." I also told him that I was willing to spend $3.5 million to make the yacht look brand-new again.

I gave the job of refurbishing the yacht to a Dutch group called Amels. I didn't talk to a lot of people about the job; I didn't have time. It was already December of 1987, and I wanted the work done quickly so that the yacht could spend the summer of 1988 in Atlantic City and New York.

Amels is a small outfit situated in the town of Makkum in the Friesland area of the Netherlands. I'd asked around, and they had a great reputation for doing what they promised and bringing projects in on time. I also found out firsthand that they took great pride in their work.

The *Trump Princess* is so big that getting it into the

Amels yacht yard on Lake Ijssel proved to be something of a problem. The water in the canal leading to the Amels repair shed, as it's called, had to be kept exceedingly high—so high that it threatened to flood some nearby farmland. We needed special permission from the Dutch government to keep the water at the necessary level, but that didn't prove to be a problem since the job we were bringing in was so beneficial to the local economy. Fortunately, there was never any serious flooding, despite the yacht's huge size. There were, however, more than a few tense moments, since the canal was narrow and we had only about three feet of clearance on either side.

Once they got the yacht into the shed, the Amels people moved in immediately and began to tear the whole thing apart. Their first task was to work on the hull, which was not as finely finished as it could have been. I pride myself in being a quick study, and I'd noticed on my inspection tour that the hull was obviously waffled—a result, I learned after asking around a bit, of the fact that the *Nabila* was built in a shipyard instead of a yacht yard, where there are higher standards of exterior workmanship. When I pointed that out to the Amels people, they assured me that after they had stripped the hull down to bare steel and filled in the indentations with a special puttylike substance, the yacht, even up close, would have the absolutely perfect lines it deserved.

Another change I ordered, after talking to the captain

Jeff Walker had tried to clean what was there, and there were still some small, very subtle spots that probably only I could see, but they bothered me. "This just won't do, Jeff," I said. He agreed and immediately made arrangements to have the sofas removed and re-covered.

The *Princess* arrived at Greenwich, Connecticut, on Saturday afternoon, the second of July. It looked absolutely magnificent sitting out there in Long Island Sound with all the local boats buzzing around it like bees around a hive. Even the most experienced sailors had never seen anything like it before.

Two days later, the *Princess* cruised into New York Harbor for the Independence Day celebration. On board, a beautiful dinner party was in progress. The guest list was star-studded.

The next day we took the *Princess* to Atlantic City, where it would begin its career as a tourist attraction and a bonus that would be granted to my best customers. It's impossible to generalize about high rollers. Some are loud and brash guys in flashy clothes; others are quiet, almost professorial types. Some can win or lose tens of thousands of dollars on the throw of the dice and just walk away. Others I've seen react to a loss by taking off their Rolexes, throwing them on the floor, and stomping on them. But not one of them failed to be impressed by the *Trump Princess*.

Of course, in places other than Atlantic City the *Trump Princess* also symbolized wealth and success, and on at least one occasion that proved to be a problem. Super Bowl Sunday of 1989 was a wild time. I was on the boat in Biscayne Bay, just outside of riot-torn Miami, and we were having a big pregame brunch with Don Johnson and Melanie Griffith, Liza Minnelli, and other celebrities. As game time approached and we were heading in to shore, I asked the captain, "What are all those fires over there and where exactly are we docking?"

The captain, who is English, just said, "Oh, you can't see precisely where we're docking because of the smoke and fire."

"Wait a minute," I said. "Two days ago they had a riot here that burned down half of Miami. If we dock this boat where people are protesting, you'll end up causing riots like you've never seen." Common sense dictates that you don't dock a $100 million yacht in an area where people are out of control. We sailed on to another, safer, section of the city.

The incredible thing about the yacht was that no one could look at it and not have a strong reaction. The press went absolutely wild when I first brought it to New York. I had thought that it might get a few lines in Liz Smith's column and other places. Instead, *Newsweek* ran a huge article, *New York* magazine did a cover story about the boat, and several other national publications also provided great coverage.

After a couple of years I started to think about an even bigger boat, and I actually had plans drawn for one. This is a classic example of how I keep trying to top myself. Owning the world's most magnificent yacht only made me want to get something even bigger and better.

But as much as I've enjoyed it until now, and as impressive as it's been to my casino customers, I think I'm giving up the game of who's got the best boat. The *Trump Princess*, as I write this, is up for sale. I don't need it anymore, I don't want it anymore, and, frankly, I can find better things to do with the money. It's funny how the boat seemed more appropriate to my life in the past than to my future.

NINE

BATTLING ON THE BOARDWALK

Life in Atlantic City

DOING business in Atlantic City, I sometimes feel like a general waging war on several fronts at once. Over here I have the Wall Street people, understandably worried about the bonds that provide much of the backing for my three casino-hotels. Over there I have the Casino Control Commission—and though I agree with their goal of keeping out organized crime, dealing with the CCC is usually no simple task.

And then, I must please the public. The nature of the casino business is such that there is always pressure on me to attract more and more people to my places, and then keep them there by every means possible, from big-name entertainment to lavish decor to first-rate food. Running a successful operation in Atlantic City would be tough enough under generally favorable circumstances, like those that prevailed for most of the fourteen or so years since gaming arrived on the scene. But during the last few years the market for casino gambling in the Northeast seems to have been growing very slowly. And that, of course, makes things all the tougher.

Although I still don't think of myself as a gambling czar, I've become deeply involved in Atlantic City's fortunes. My first project there was the Trump Plaza, which I built (in partnership, for a time, with Holiday Inns) in the early 1980s. Then I opened the Trump Castle, a facility I took over from Hilton after that company failed to obtain a gaming license from the CCC. In 1989 I bought the Trump Regency and a prime piece of property on which Bob Guccione had started building a hotel—relatively low-profile but, I think, interesting deals that I'll get into in the next chapter. Finally, in April of 1990, I opened the city's crown jewel, the Taj Mahal, my ultimate sign of faith in the venerable resort town.

A fact that's gotten lost in all of the adverse publicity I encountered in 1990 is that, on the whole, my Atlantic City ventures have been extremely successful. Running them, though, has never been easy, for the reasons I've already stated, and because of the cost of borrowing the money I needed to build and expand. I had to begin consolidating my operations and, more to the point, renegotiating some of the bank loans that had been offered so freely.

But despite those tough times, I remain extremely optimistic about Atlantic City, and I'll tell you why.

If the town can draw tens of millions of people and generate many billions in revenues and tax dollars at a time when there is so much about the area that seems designed to keep people out, or even drive them away, think of what will happen when improvements are made. Or maybe I should say *if* they are made. As confident as I am about the potential growth of the Atlantic City market, I've seen too much of the local politics and waited too long for the emergence of a visionary thinker. Hopefully, the new mayor, James Whelan, will be that person.

I can dazzle you with charts detailing the town's positive impact on the state economy; I can produce graphs showing the number of jobs that have been created by the gaming industry. But if anyone ever expresses any doubts about Atlantic City's potential in my presence, I prefer to tell him or her about an irate letter I received not long ago from a man who had traveled down to Trump Castle by helicopter from New York.

Along the way, it seems, the pilot announced that he'd detected a possible minor problem and, just to be safe, he was bringing the helicopter down in rural New Jersey to check things out. It must have been an unsettling experience for all concerned, even though, fortunately, everything turned out fine. But what this letter writer was absolutely livid about was not the unscheduled landing. No, he was furious because the delay had cost him several hours of precious casino time.

That kind of enthusiasm for Atlantic City is far from rare. It's easy for people who've never been there to forget, in all the talk about a "softening" market, that crowds of people continue to pour in, by bus, by car, by helicopter, and—to the extent they can, given the current airport conditions—by plane, from almost everywhere east of the Mississippi. In terms of the tourist visits it generates, Atlantic City is the number-one travel destination in America—bigger than Las Vegas, Orlando, or, believe it or not, New York City. No one who walks along the world-famous Boardwalk on a Saturday night in summer—or whenever a big fight is in town—can fail to be impressed by the scene: the flashing lights, the carnival noise, and huge crowds streaming in and out of the casino doors. During the height of the season the energy level is incredible and the town is booked solid. And, of course, the money comes streaming in to corporate and state coffers— all of it from people who are having a fabulously good time and who are extremely likely, the research shows, to return.

That's my definition of a healthy situation. The problem in Atlantic City has been that the off-season is *too* off. The area, if it's going to be truly successful, needs to generate customers on a year-round basis. But before we can get significant numbers of people to visit the town when weather conditions are less than ideal and the airlines are advertising bargain fares to Florida, radical changes are in order.

A trip to Atlantic City needs to be made more attractive—to gamblers and nongamblers alike. That's a simple idea and not a very controversial one. I don't think anyone has ever disagreed with me when I make the point that if there is something for the kids to do, the whole family will come and stay several nights in our hotels. Right now most of the casino customers are daytrippers who don't think of the town as a true vacation spot and, as a result, aren't contributing to the local economy as much as they might. You can bus down more senior citizens or put up more billboards till you drop, but making the area multifaceted is the key to gaining a breakthrough to a new, more prosperous era.

Yet turning Atlantic City into a real resort town is something no one casino operator, however successful or influential, can do. And finding an elected or appointed official who is both sharp enough and powerful enough to turn things around has so far proved impossible. I believe, however, that the newly elected governor of New Jersey, Jim Florio, with his great drive and imagination, will do great things for Atlantic

City. But I have to say that the story of Atlantic City, up to this point, is a story of missed opportunities.

The most basic opportunity that's been missed is a chance to rid the town of blight and urban decay. More than a decade after the passage of legalized casino gambling, Atlantic City remains a hodgepodge of fantastic hotels and dilapidated old houses. Everyone who arrives via the Atlantic City Expressway, the main route into town, says the same thing: The contrast between the old Atlantic City and the new is very striking—and depressing. Yet what was holding the town back in 1976 is still holding it back today. Those involved in the town are trying to sell Atlantic City as a luxury resort. But you can't compete with the south of France when you've got the South Bronx around most every corner.

The maddening thing is that there's really no excuse for the way the town has developed.

The fact is, this is *not* the South Bronx or any typically depressed urban area that we are talking about. Atlantic City represents a unique situation; it is like no other town in America. In most places you'll find ideas but not enough money to carry them out. In Atlantic City there is plenty of money, but there are almost no ideas—only, in the past, political corruption and cronyism.

Atlantic City has money because of a fund that was set up years ago and into which every hotel-casino operator has been dutifully paying. Hundreds of millions of dollars have gone into that so-called Casino Reinvestment Development Authority, but all that has come out of it so far is some low-income housing so badly designed and poorly situated that people don't want to live in it.

I was speaking with a friend at the Disney Company recently, and during the course of our conversation he asked if I had ever considered building a Disney World-type attraction in Atlantic City. I took out a map and showed it to him. "What is that dot?" he asked. "A housing project," I said. "And that one?" he asked. Of course it was another housing project.

He got the point—which is that you're never going to turn Atlantic City into a full-fledged fantasyland as long as you've got these pockets of poverty all over town.

Certainly, most poor people want to better themselves, and they should be given not just a chance but real help to do so. But no one, rich or poor, wants to raise children in a neighborhood devoted to gambling, because of all the problems gambling brings. Do underprivileged people really want to live side-by-side with casinos? Look at the record: Much of the housing that's gone up in Atlantic City during the last few years has been very hard to fill.

A lot of the rules that hotel operators have to follow don't make sense in a town that's trying to create an atmosphere of escape and fantasy. For example, I can build a $1 billion hotel with entranceways featuring fabulous gardens and fountains. But if a hot dog vendor wants to park a filthy broken-down cart in front of my place, there's nothing I can do about it.

Atlantic City is really an island, and we need to develop it as an island resort, cut off from the realities of everyday life and devoted exclusively to recreation. The huge amounts of money in the Casino Reinvestment Development Authority should be used to put in green areas, shopping districts, and attractions that will appeal to all sorts of vacationers from all age groups. The casinos should also subsidize housing for the poor—but good housing, situated in outlying towns, where people want to live and maintain families.

The Casino Control Commission is the organization charged with regulating the industry in the city. I will say right up front that these people are doing a great job. Mob influence in Atlantic City is, as far as I can tell, nil. While the CCC's motives are beyond question, the fact remains that Atlantic City is still a long way from what it could be.

Look at the situation in Las Vegas. In that town, when the Hilton Corporation wants to build an extra thousand rooms on one of its buildings, the local officials practically erect a monument to the company.

The authorities out there have a very different attitude. They encourage you to build; there's a real esprit de corps—a feeling that everyone is working together.

The attitude of the press in the two towns is also very different. In Las Vegas there are two papers, both of them very upbeat. The media out there are geared to accentuating the positive and criticizing constructively. In Atlantic City the press in many respects does a great job, but its basic view of the gaming business is often negative to the point of being hostile.

Atlantic City's other key need is for an airport capable of handling major airline traffic. At the moment there are two landing strips not far from town, but neither is equipped for the kinds of planes that should be bringing in gambling junketeers and other vacationers by the thousands. When people ask me, "Is an airport *really* necessary?" I respond by saying, "Try to imagine Las Vegas without one."

The state will have to come up with the funds for airport expansion, though, and that could be a long and frustrating process. It takes guts for a politician to stand up and put forth the idea that making an investment in Atlantic City now will mean more tax revenue for senior citizens, low-income housing, and a host of other social programs down the road. It will be interesting to see whether, in a state that is still coming to grips with the fact that it is a major gambling center, anyone rises to the occasion.

Because of all the improvements that need to be made in Atlantic City, the contrasts—between rich and poor, between the off-season and the warmer months—will endure. But I'm confident that I'll do well. I have the best facilities and great locations. And I also understand that, as tough as times get, the key to success in the casino-hotel business, as in a lot of other areas, is to carry on as if *these* are the good old days.

Even in relatively slow times, you have to keep improving your facilities by constantly plowing a large part of your profits back into their operation. At Trump Plaza, I added the sumptuous Central Park garage at a cost of more than $30 million. I could have built a perfectly functional no-frills facility for a lot less, of course, but I felt the extra expense was worth it if I could beautify the area while I was providing badly needed parking spaces. In the last few years I've spent another $60 million or so refurbishing the interior of the hotel and improving the façades of the stores located throughout the hotel.

Over at the Castle, meanwhile, we put in a magnificent marina, added suites, and built a new wing called the Crystal Tower. I've invested many millions of dollars in that property since I purchased it from Barron Hilton.

What even a lot of casino operators never realize about Atlantic City is that people who come there don't generally respond to price-slashing promotions and other bargain come-ons, which always have the look of desperation about them. Rather, the casino customers like things that symbolize success.

A few years ago one of my competitors began a very expensive ad campaign that spoke to the blue-collar guy and said, in effect, "We're your kind of place."

A huge mistake. I'm all for blue-collar workers. I respect them as people, I need them as customers, and I appreciate their business just as much as that of the high rollers. But the fact is that every blue-collar worker wants to be treated like a high roller, not like an ordinary guy. These people gravitate toward the symbols of success; they want to *touch* success. Knowing this, I wasn't surprised when that blue-collar ad campaign turned out to be a total failure, doing permanent damage to the image of the hotel that ran the spot.

I won't pretend to know exactly what's ultimately going to happen to Atlantic City—but it has a chance to be something terrific.

TEN

PLAYBOY AND PENTHOUSE
A Good Pair

IN 1989 the problems that have plagued Atlantic City since its rebirth came to a head. Several of the twelve casino-hotels lost money, and for the first time since gambling came to the town, one place—the Atlantis—was forced to close.

It didn't thrill me to see that happen. On the other hand, I was on the phone negotiating to buy the troubled hotel as soon as I thought the moment was right.

Why would I want to buy a place in Atlantic City at a time when the market was starting to go slack?

For two reasons.

The first was that the slump had yet to hit my properties. (In fact, for all the bad publicity I've received, it still hasn't affected me as much as it has most of the other casino operators.) The Trump Plaza at that point had an occupancy rate of about 92 percent, which meant that the only times rooms were available was during the middle of the week in the off-season. During the peak periods, we were turning away at least four customers for every one we were able to handle. And the thought of that pained me greatly.

The second reason is that when I see a potential bargain, I instinctively move in.

I'd had my eye on the Atlantis practically since it was first opened, by Hugh Hefner, as the Playboy Casino Hotel in 1981. The place had always struck me as a good-looking failure. Certainly for Hefner it was a total disaster. When he couldn't get a gaming license—in part because the Casino Control Commission uncovered allegations that the manager of his New York Playboy Club might have violated some rules of the state liquor authority twenty years before—he was forced to close. It was a huge blow to the whole Playboy empire, and one that could have been avoided, or at least softened, if he'd gotten his approvals in order before he started construction. In any case, Hefner eventually sold out to his partner in the project, the Elsinore Corporation of Chicago, and the hotel was reopened as the Atlantis.

The hotel's first big problem was its name. As I've said before, giving yourself the right image is extremely important in the casino business, and the name sets the tone for your place. There are no rules about picking a name; some work and some don't.

"Trump," fortunately, has sent the right message. "Atlantis," on the other hand, just didn't say excitement, stability, or success.

Another problem that Elsinore faced was the three-level casino that Hefner had designed into his facility. The original idea was to suggest a private English club by having gaming tables on several floors. In a way, Playboy should be commended for trying to do something different in an industry which is regulated to the point of stultifying sameness. But in practice, people just didn't like waiting for an elevator to go from, say, the slot machines to the 21 tables—and it didn't make them feel any better to know that this is what the in-crowd does in London.

To make matters even worse, Elsinore did a poor job of marketing its place. The high rollers never went near the Atlantis, and neither did a lot of the $500-to-$1,000 players, who can be a casino's bread and butter. By the end of their tenure as owners, the Elsinore people were so desperate to attract customers that they were offering bus riders more in meal coupons and other bonuses than those people could possibly generate. The casino was actually losing money on everyone who took advantage of its overly generous promotions.

It wasn't any secret that the Atlantis was floundering. I have a habit of asking people—limo drivers, corporate executives, Atlantic City insiders—what they think of an idea I'm considering at any given time. Usually, I get a lot of different opinions. But whenever I'd bounce the idea of buying the Atlantis off people, their response was always the same: They'd tell me it was a sure winner—for the right price.

The Atlantis happened to be a beautiful twenty-two-story, five-hundred-room hotel located on the other side of the Convention Center from the Trump Plaza. If it could be operated as a non-casino hotel, under a different name, it was almost certain, I felt, to be a success.

That's why I listened closely when, on several occasions, representatives of Elsinore called to see if I might be interested in buying the property.

In the end, though, for all their eagerness to sell, the price they put on the property was always unreasonably high. Elsinore didn't know how to run the place, or how to get rid of it, either. And so the status quo remained and the losses mounted. At one point several years ago, the Atlantis actually went bankrupt, only to emerge from the process and immediately resume its losing ways. By April 1989, the Casino Control commissioners had apparently seen enough to convince them that the hotel was on extremely shaky financial ground.

Since it was a matter of public record that the Atlantis had lost more than $65 million the previous year, the announcement of its probable demise came as no great surprise. Still, this would be the first time an Atlantic City casino was forced to close, and the news had a sobering effect, not just within the town but in other communities that perhaps had seen the passage of gambling legislation as the instant answer to all their financial worries. The fact is, gambling is not a panacea; it creates as many problems for a community as it solves.

For example, with the closing of the Atlantis, more than two thousand employees were in danger of losing their jobs. What's more, if a buyer did not come along quickly, a town that desperately needed rooms would find itself losing five hundred of them—and gaining a boarded-up and forlorn-looking monument to failure.

Even by the projections of its own vice president for finance, the Atlantis would, if all went well, have only two thousand dollars more than the legal minimum required to keep its doors open. If things went slightly worse than expected and someone·won big, the casino might not have enough money to pay off that customer. An independent analyst that the CCC brought in took one look at the situation and told the commissioners that the Atlantis was "running on water."

It was only a matter of time, I knew, before I'd get a phone call from an Elsinore representative offering me a deal on the Atlantis. In one sense I wasn't their best prospect, because with the purchase of the Taj, still unfinished at the time, I had already reached the limit of three casino licenses allowed to any one individual or company under state law. If I bought the

Atlantis, it would be for the rooms and convention space only, and thus its value would be less to me than to someone who would run it as a casino-hotel.

On the other hand, I was virtually the only investor then in the market for important properties in Atlantic City. If they sold to me, they'd get something in exchange for their hotel. If they waited until a conservator took control, they might never see a dime of the sales price. Rather than do that, they would probably close down, a move that would put a lot of Atlantis people out of work and otherwise damage the local economy.

When the call from Elsinore came, I let Harvey Freeman handle it. By staying out of the initial discussions, I also was able to create the impression of aloofness, which in this case worked in my favor. After all, it was Elsinore that was being pressured to make a move, not me.

Their first price, as reported to me by Harvey, was lower than it had been in previous discussions. Still, it was considerably more than I thought we could get it for. "Let's just sit tight," I told Harvey. "We'll wait for them to get back to us."

Which they did—at six-thirty in the evening on Friday, April 14. The timing was significant: The day before, the CCC had appointed a well-known New Jersey lawyer named Joseph Nolan to become conservator of the Atlantis casino. In taking this step, the CCC ruled that Nolan's fee of $15,000 a month should be paid from the Atlantis cash reserve—and that the conservator should assume control at the stroke of midnight on April 14.

I was in my apartment when Harvey called and said the Elsinore people had reached him at home and said they wanted to work a deal in the next few hours. I had done some thinking about what the property was worth to me, and I had a number ready. "Let's offer them $61 million," I said to Harvey. He agreed, but suggested that we put in $2 million more that would be earmarked for some Atlantis creditors whom we would be counting on to supply food and other goods if and when we took over. "We don't want those people mad at us," Harvey said. All in all, it was a very good price, considering that it had cost $159 million to build the hotel in 1981.

About two hours later, Harvey called me back again and said we had a deal. In the interim he had contacted my lawyers from Dreyer & Traub, and he suggested that we meet in their offices, on Park Avenue and Fortieth Street, at 11:00 P.M. Some Elsinore lawyers would meet us there, he said, and we could hash out a few last-minute details and fax the signed agreement to the offices of Elsinore in Chicago by the midnight deadline.

Unfortunately, when you're dealing with a property in Atlantic City, things can never be that simple. In New York I could buy a hotel like the St. Moritz, sell it for a profit of substantially more than $100 million, put the money in the bank, and go on to the next deal without ever being bothered about licensing. But when everything you do has to be approved by a Casino Control Commission, you have to proceed with caution.

Even though I wouldn't be using the Atlantis as a gambling facility, I wanted to make sure that the commission didn't look askance at my owning another Boardwalk property. "If I'm going to jeopardize my gaming license for this, it's not worth it," I told Harvey. I suggested he call a certain member of the CCC and get an advance reading of the commission's likely attitude toward the transaction before I signed anything. About half an hour later, Harvey called back again and said that, while this man made it clear that he could not speak officially, he didn't see anything objectionable about our purchase of the Atlantis. Although there was always the risk that the full commission could adopt an entirely different attitude, that did make me feel better.

Harvey was really on edge throughout the final negotiations. As our lawyers talked to their lawyers about minor details, the clock kept ticking, and he kept reminding everyone of the midnight deadline. "It really doesn't matter as long as we have an agreement in principle before midnight," one of the Elsinore lawyers said. "Bullshit," Harvey snapped back. "Let's get this thing on the wire before the deadline." It was exactly 11:58 P.M. when the fax of our agreement went out to Chicago.

As it turned out, Harvey was right to be so concerned about the timing. As soon as we announced that we'd reached an agreement to buy the Atlantis, Joseph Nolan, the conservator, who was supposed to take over the property at 12:01 A.M., went wild. Suddenly there was no need for a conservator, and he obviously didn't like that. I don't know whether he was madder about losing his fee or his moment in the sun, but he spent an amazing amount of time and energy trying to convince the CCC that they should invalidate the Atlantis sale. He claimed that the price was too low; he said that he should have been consulted during the negotiations; and he even tried to prove that the commission had made a clerical error and the deadline for the Atlantis sale should have been twenty-four hours earlier.

Fortunately, I did have support in my dispute with the would-be conservator. The CCC's own Division of Gaming Enforcement studied the matter and dismissed each of Nolan's objections, saying that I had a valid agreement, signed on time and at a fair price. At around the same time, representatives of Atlantis employees and creditors also went before the commission to ask that it approve my deal. A lawyer from the Hotel Employees and Restaurant Employees International Union pointed out that if there was any delay in the process and the Atlantis was forced to close completely, some 850 workers would lose their jobs.

Meanwhile, I had already let it be known, in an interview with the *Newark Star-Ledger*, that it was highly unlikely that I'd go through with the deal if the hotel was forced to close. It would cost tens of millions of dollars to recruit a new hotel staff from scratch, I said. And besides, it would be ten times harder to make a success of a hotel that had been shut down and boarded up than of one that had never lost its momentum.

A few days later, the commission declared my purchase of the Atlantis valid but stopped short of issuing a final approval. The problem now, they said, was that they needed to study another question—whether my holdings in the city, including the Penthouse site which I had just acquired, amounted to an excessive "economic concentration."

Naturally, Nolan was in the thick of the argument again, saying that ownership of the Atlantis, when added to my other holdings, would give me "an undue economic concentration of meeting space, hotel rooms, parking space, and perhaps other aspects of the casino-hotel business in Atlantic City."

Clearly, I was a major investor in Atlantic City. But should I be the object of suspicion because of that? Again, here I was trying to keep a major hotel from closing, to invest $20 million in its renovation, and to preserve hundreds of jobs—and all I was getting in return was a hard time.

When the CCC finally gave its unanimous approval to the Atlantis deal, on June 16, 1989, I considered it a great victory, particularly because the CCC had concluded that my Atlantis and Penthouse acquisitions would have a positive effect on economic development in Atlantic City. A few days before, an independent economic analyst hired by the Division of Gaming Enforcement, Professor Carl Shapiro of the Woodrow Wilson School of Public and International Affairs of Princeton University, had supported my position, saying that the purchase of the hotel in no way violated any antitrust considerations and was, in fact, vastly preferable to having the town lose five hundred rooms.

The CCC, in issuing its approval, did impose three restrictions on me. The commission said I must seek prior permission before building any more hotel rooms, buying any more casino-zoned land, or acquiring any interest in a company with a casino license. But I can handle these restrictions. Besides, as Commissioner Kenneth Burdge noted, "If the time comes that Mr. Trump needs additional property to expand any of his casinos due to the competitive nature of his business, he should be able to do so."

That wasn't the end of this particular war, though. The sale of the Atlantis was still before a federal bankruptcy judge named Rosemary Gambardella in Camden, New Jersey, and whatever happened in that court was crucial. My friend Joseph Nolan was battling us there, too. Acting perhaps out of a desire to save his conservator job, he had come up with about nine other parties who he said were interested in making bids for the Atlantis. One offer that he said exceeded mine came from the Nakash brothers, who made a lot of money selling Jordache jeans. His list of investors also included TV talk-show host Morton Downey, Jr.; a Kansas real estate firm; and a Long Island investor who said in his statement that he was bidding for the "Atlantic" hotel. It was in the interest of the Atlantis creditors, Nolan maintained, that every one of these other proposals should be considered alongside that of Donald Trump.

I honestly couldn't have agreed more, and I told my lawyers not to stand in Nolan's way and to do everything to speed the bankruptcy process along. The way I looked at it, if my deal didn't have the endorsement of Judge Gambardella, I'd be in court for years, fending off all kinds of potential buyers and frustrated former creditors. The situation reminded me of what I went through to buy the Eastern Shuttle. Because I let it be known that I would not raise my offer by even one dollar, I was taking the risk of losing everything I'd fought so hard for. But I wanted the Atlantis free and clear and on my terms—or not at all.

The tension was palpable in the courtroom just before Judge Gambardella announced her decision. Finally, the purchase was approved, "free and clear of all liens, claims and encumbrances of whatsoever kind or nature.'' She described my no-strings, all-cash offer as ''higher and better'' than any of the others, which were contingent on financing and various kinds of CCC approvals.

There was nothing more to say. I had my beautiful five-hundred-room hotel, now known as the Trump Regency. Nolan, meanwhile, had no choice but to tender his resignation.

The Penthouse Affair

The story of how I acquired the Penthouse property is still unfolding as I write.

Like the Atlantis, the Penthouse property was something that had been on my mind for a long time. It consists of a plot of land and a superstructure adjoining the Trump Plaza, the most successful hotel-casino in town other than the Taj Mahal.

In fact, it was nothing more than an underutilized eyesore—a stark steel skeleton of what was supposed to have been the Penthouse Hotel and Casino.

Bob Guccione's dream of making it big in Atlantic City had come to a grinding halt in 1979. Why the successful publisher of *Penthouse* magazine ever wanted to build in Atlantic City in the first place is something of a mystery to me. My best guess is that he started construction because in the late seventies, at the height of the skin-magazine wars, Hugh Hefner had announced that Playboy was building a casino-hotel in Atlantic City. Guccione, I've since learned, is an extremely driven, competitive guy, and he probably didn't want to just sit back and watch his biggest rival get involved in a potentially lucrative and glamorous venture.

Like Hefner, though, rumor has it, Guccione was stymied by the CCC, which let it be known, far in advance of any actual hearing, that for some reason he wasn't easily going to be licensed.

When Guccione got the word that he wouldn't qualify, he simply stopped building and busied himself with other matters. I'm sure he was glad, in a way, to be done with something that had been plagued with problems from the start. After much expenditure of time, effort, and money, Guccione had never been able to assemble the complete site on which to build his hotel. One owner of a small old house held out on him, demanding millions of dollars for a piece of property that was probably worth a few thousand before casino gambling hit town. Bob had no choice but to design his hotel around the holdout as best he could. Finally, he gave up on the project. Since his property sat at the very entrance to the city, what this meant was that visitors rolled off the Atlantic City Expressway and immediately saw a mishmash of dilapidated homes and rusting steel girders.

That wasn't good for either the town or for Guccione, who was paying about $8 million a year in carrying charges on the property. He never seemed very interested in selling it, though, judging by his cool response whenever one of my employees would call his organization and ask about the site's availability. After a while a rumor started to the effect that Guccione and I were feuding. Bob hated me, I heard, because of my numerous successes in Atlantic City, a town that had not exactly welcomed him with open arms. I could see why some people would think that, after years went by and a deal that would have been mutually beneficial never got made.

I think the truth was that Bob, normally a very shrewd guy, simply tuned out the Atlantic City scene until he got sick of owning that expensive piece of property. In time, he agreed to sell it to the Pratt Hotel Corporation.

Jack Pratt, the president of the company, had told Guccione that Pratt Hotel would be able to build a $300 million hotel-casino on the Penthouse property. In the end that didn't happen—but of course no one knew that yet.

When I first heard what Pratt was planning, I was more than a little concerned because he had absolutely no provision for on-site parking. In a city that was already suffering from a severe shortage of parking spaces and had traffic congestion approaching that of midtown Manhattan, this seemed foolish beyond belief.

There was no way I was going to let Pratt get his zoning and CCC approvals for a project that was going to cause major traffic problems for Trump Plaza and Atlantic City. I wasted no time in informing the proper authorities that Pratt's plan was a disaster waiting to happen. Caesars Hotel joined me in objecting to Pratt's plan and in urging the zoning board to withhold approval for the project.

However, Pratt managed to get the approval from the zoning board. I appealed that decision, but in the end it didn't matter because Pratt didn't close the deal.

Pratt originally had until December 15, 1988, to come up with the purchase price, according to their agreement, which included a "time is of the essence" clause. What that meant was that there could be no valid reason for going beyond the designated date. As it turned out, however, Penthouse did grant a forty-five-day extension, which moved the deadline to February 1. Pratt did not meet that deadline either.

My negotiations for the Penthouse property were concluded in mid-March. Each of us was getting what he wanted, and so we settled on a price of $35 million and Penthouse and the Trump Organization announced the agreement. Because the deal would bring major improvements to a key area of Atlantic City, everyone in town was happy—except the Pratt Hotel Corporation. It immediately issued a statement saying that it would "vigorously pursue legal remedies against the Trump Organization and Penthouse International." This despite the fact that they never had the money to build the proposed hotel and repeatedly failed or were unable to purchase the site regardless of the two deadlines.

As things worked out, however, Penthouse sued first, seeking to compel Pratt to comply with various contractual obligations. Pratt threatened that he would "sue Trump like he's never been sued before." And he was right. On April 3, 1989, he sued me and Bob Guccione, as well as the companies we head, for everything from conspiracy to fraud to racketeering. Since the case is still pending as I write this, my lawyers have told me not to comment on it any further. To do so would be in bad taste and unethical. The unfortunate thing is that because of this suit I am unable to clean up the main entryway to Atlantic City, creating not only hotel rooms but beautiful parks, vistas, and open spaces. Instead, gutted, blighted buildings now stand as sad reminders of Atlantic City's problems.

This is where Leona Helmsley enters the story.

As luck would have it, one of the parcels of land that composed the Penthouse site was owned by Leona Helmsley and her wonderful husband, Harry, the legendary New York real estate man. As part of our deal, I'd acquired a long-term lease on the parcel with an option to purchase, but I needed to obtain the landlord's formal consent before I could exercise the option. In ninety-nine out of a hundred cases this is a mere formality, and in fact Leona was contractually bound to give her consent unless there was an important reason for her to withhold it. She, however, chose not to cooperate, and because of her, my whole deal was being delayed and possibly jeopardized for no good reason.

When Leona pulled this stunt I was mad as hell—but not in the least surprised. This is a vindictive woman who, in a few years, has virtually destroyed the reputation that Harry, over the course of a lifetime, built up.

My relationship with Leona dates back many years, to the time when I was a young guy just starting out in real estate. For some reason, even though I was not tremendously successful at that time, Leona always liked having me around. Whenever she gave one of her "I'm Just Wild About Harry" parties for her husband, I was always asked to be there and was always given a great seat, usually right near her. It was a strange situation to be in: I could see hostility in her eyes, but for a long time none of it was directed toward me. In fact, she went around telling everybody that "this young man will be the next Harry Helmsley," that I was the smartest of the smart, and that there was nobody to compete with me.

I was very flattered. At the same time I knew Leona had a hair-trigger temper and was ready to explode at any time.

One night about fifteen years ago, when I was still a bachelor, I attended one of her parties with a young and very attractive fashion model as my date. As soon as Leona saw who was with me, she became incensed. "How dare you bring that tramp to one of my parties?" she screamed, looking the girl directly in the eyes.

At first I was shocked, but then all the things people had been telling me about Leona and her Jekyll-and-Hyde personality started coming back to me. The rest of the evening Leona was all smiles and small talk, as if nothing had happened.

The next day, when I was in my office, she called and said, "You fucking son-of-a-bitch. I watched you politicking the room and all of my guests in order to get your convention center passed. Don't do that on my time. And don't bring pretty girls to my parties anymore, especially girls that make the other women in the room look like shit." She then screamed over the phone, "Fuck you," and hung up.

Welcome to the world of Leona Helmsley.

As the years went by, Leona became obsessed with me. The situation became so bad that once, at a small dinner party, she stood up, apropos of nothing, and explained to everyone what a bad guy Donald Trump was. My friends at the party couldn't believe the spectacle they were hearing and seeing.

Because of the business Leona and I were in, our paths would often cross, and each time she would stare at me angrily—I was never sure why. On two occasions she actually gave me the finger across a crowded New York ballroom. Once, at some social function, someone made the mistake of asking her if she knew me, and she flew into such a rage that the poor guy had to gather up his wife and go home.

Of course I had my ways of getting even with her. During the period when she was hardly speaking to me, I was instrumental in breaking up the so-called Tudor City land swap, which would have allowed Leona to build a luxury apartment house or a hotel on what is now a park across from the United Nations. It was a moment of sweet revenge.

Our period of estrangement went on for five or six years. Whenever I'd see Harry, he'd be unbelievably nice to me. But if Leona was around, he'd pretend I didn't exist. Harry was truly intimidated in his later years by her crazed personality.

It wasn't always that way. One evening years ago, Harry and Leona were having dinner with me, and Leona was in a particularly obnoxious mood, screaming at the waiters to the point of being out of control. Toward the middle of the evening Harry got up, slammed the table, and shouted, "Leona, that's enough. You're out of order. You will be quiet for the rest of the evening." She was like a lamb from then on.

Unfortunately, as time went by, Harry's strength and will began to disappear, and Leona started getting away with things that a younger Harry would never have allowed.

She was like no one I'd ever met. I'll never forget

a conversation I had with her when her only son, Jay Panzirer, died of a heart attack. I had read that Harry was creating a foundation in memory of Jay, and I decided to send a check in honor of Harry. A couple of days later I got a phone call from Leona. "You fucking son-of-a-bitch," she started, as usual, "this was the nicest thing that I could ever imagine you doing." She then began to cry.

I didn't know what to say. Then, toward the end of the conversation, the tears totally disappeared, and she screamed at me, "But it proves one thing—you're not as smart as I thought." I didn't know what she was talking about until she went on, "If you'd sent it through a corporation, instead of sending it personally, you would have gotten a tax deduction on the money." I told Leona that the check was not sent for that purpose, and the phone call ended nicely.

Some months later a major New York City bank was having a dinner at the Metropolitan Museum of Art. I found myself sitting at a table with the Helmsleys. Because of our last telephone call, things were extremely cordial between us, but Leona soon was out of control. The banker who was assigned to our table took tremendous abuse from Leona, who shouted at him that if he didn't "behave," she would make Harry take all of his money out of this man's bank, "and we'll leave your bank in a shambles."

Leona then looked at Ivana, who had said earlier that she was getting ready to take the kids on a vacation without me because I was too busy to go. "You're a fool to leave your husband alone in New York," she shouted at Ivana. "I haven't left Harry for one night during our entire marriage, and I never will."

About that, I have to admit, Leona may have been right.

But no one is capable of getting along with Leona for an extended period of time—especially no one who is successful. She is a jealous, unhappy woman who will not allow herself the luxury of having friends. Even when our relationship was relatively civil, I remember thinking, I just hope I never need anything from her. Unfortunately, the day came when I had to ask for her official consent on that parcel of land in Atlantic City.

Although such a request should have resulted in a routine approval, I knew that nothing would be routine if Leona Helmsley found out I was buying this land. Interestingly, I had seen Leona only days before at the Plaza Hotel, at a function where she and Harry were being honored. At that time she was as nice as she could be, bestowing hugs and kisses on me enthusiastically. Nevertheless, what should have been an easy okay turned out to be a major event.

One night during the time that Leona was digging in her heels, I attended a birthday party for one of New York's truly wonderful people, developer Lew Rudin. At the party was a man named Irving Schneider, who worked with Harry Helmsley. I didn't know him, but his reputation was that of a hard, mean-spirited man who, like Leona, seemed to enjoy inflicting pain.

When I saw Irving, he began telling me what a wonderful job I was doing. I thanked him and then asked, "Where is my approval on the land in Atlantic City?"

He said, "The lawyers will be in touch with you," which meant that I was not going to get the approval and that it would have to be worked out in court.

I looked at him and said, "You tell that woman you work for that I look forward to suing her ass off, and that by the time I finish with her, lots of people in this city will be very happy."

I thought he'd be happy to get this message, because I'd heard that Leona abused Irving Schneider the way she abused Harry. Instead, he went wild. "Who the hell do you think you are?" he asked. And for the first time since high school, I found myself challenged to a fight. "I ought to take you outside and show you who's boss," he said.

"Well, that would be all right with me, I guess," I said with a shrug, "if that's what you'd like to do." He then started screaming that I had challenged him to a fight and that I had threatened him. I'll never forget watching this man at the bar, unable to lift a drink to his mouth after having made a complete fool of himself. The funny part is that despite his constantly kissing Leona's ass, she treated him like dirt.

The next day I wrote a stinging letter to Leona Helmsley and sent a copy to every newspaper in the New York area.

That letter became a huge story in the next day's papers; the *New York Post*, in fact, put it on the front page. Largely as a result of that publicity, Leona totally backed down, and I received the consent.

Which goes to show that the best way to deal with a bully is head-on.

ELEVEN

IRON MIKE
AND ME

I love sports, but I hated being a team owner. The New Jersey Generals—with Herschel Walker, Doug Flutie, and Brian Sipe—were definitely a class act of the short-lived United States Football League. Still, watching them from the owner's box every week was just too much of a roller-coaster ride. When they won, I felt great. When they lost, however, my emotions took a dive and I walked around feeling lousy until the following Sunday. I hate losing. But when I have no direct control over whether I'm winning or getting beat, I find the situation intolerable.

Boxing is different. Boxing, for one thing, is not a clubby network like the National Football League. In many ways, it's a very simple, very raw business. If you've got the money to lay out for a big match, you can get involved on the highest levels almost instantly. These days, of course, that's a pretty big "if." The so-called site fees for major fights have escalated to the point of being almost ridiculous. Even a less-than-earthshaking bout can cost $10 million or more.

Which leads me to the second thing I like about boxing: It allows me to exercise my business instincts. There's no national governing body, no league, virtually no structure of any kind. *I'm* the one who decides which matches to go after and which to pass on, how to deal with the various promoters, and then how to manage and market the event so I come out ahead. Staging a big boxing match is like roaring down the road in a very hot sports car, steering and shifting as you negotiate the curves. It's downright nerve-racking at times but, ultimately, great fun.

What I *don't* like about boxing is that it is a business in which there are very few bargains. These days, it's almost impossible not to overpay at least somewhat for a major fight. That's because boxing is no longer a business that has to make sense at the box office. Today the big matches all wind up at casino-hotels, usually either at the Trump Plaza or the Taj Mahal in Atlantic City, or some place in Las Vegas. Casino-hotels can afford to merely break even, or even to lose a little money on ticket sales, because a major boxing match often brings with it a huge army of gamblers who line the tables six deep—and don't go home until they've won or lost a great deal of money.

Notice I said that the gamblers "often" show up; I didn't say "always." Sometimes a casino owner will overestimate the appeal of a particular fight and wind up losing many millions. The Mike Tyson-Frank Bruno fight of a few years ago is a case in point. Another hotel bought that fight for a reported $5 million, and in one sense I can't blame them for thinking it was worth a lot. Tyson-Bruno came just a few months after the successful matchup between Tyson and Michael Spinks—a bout staged, by the way, at the Trump Plaza in Atlantic City. Although it was not exactly a masterpiece of athletic competition, the Tyson-Spinks bout was one of the great *events* of the eighties. What else, inside or outside the world of sports, made the covers of *Time, Life, People*, and *Sports Illustrated* and got extensive coverage on prime-time network TV? Coming on the heels of that huge success, Tyson-Bruno looked to a lot of people like a can't-miss event. I, however, passed on the bout, feeling that after watching Mike knock out Spinks in ninety-one seconds, the public wasn't in the mood for another one-sided spectacle. That was just an educated guess, based on no scientific marketing surveys, but as it turned out, I was right. According to the newspaper reports, it was necessary to give away thousands of dollars' worth of tickets so their arena would look filled up on TV.

I wouldn't be involved in boxing if I didn't believe I have good gut instincts for the sport. It's just too risky a business otherwise. But in boxing, as in any other field, you don't develop instincts without doing a lot of homework. I read the sports pages every day and keep tabs on how certain fights did on pay-per-view and network TV. I also keep in touch with a lot of streetwise people—the kind you don't find on Wall Street, Fifth Avenue, or, for that matter, anywhere outside the strange world of professional boxing.

The most interesting boxer of all, in my opinion, is a former Brooklyn street kid named Mike Tyson—the once and, I believe, future champion of the world.

Mike had a run of fame such as no one else, except perhaps the great Muhammad Ali, has ever had. For a brief but shining period, he looked absolutely superhuman. He was more than just a great boxer. He was one of the most talked-about people in the world.

I can still remember standing in the grand ballroom of the Plaza Hotel in New York about a month or two before the Buster Douglas fight and watching Mike make an elaborate entrance with his promoter Don King. The occasion was a dinner to benefit the March of Dimes. Ivana had been responsible for putting together the guest list, and at one point she had mentioned to me that although the evening included all the big names from the New York social scene and a host of other celebrities, it lacked some special excitement, something that would set it apart from similar events.

I suggested she invite Mike. One phone call from her was all it took to get the heavyweight champ and Don King to come in from Cleveland. Both said they were happy to help raise money for the March of Dimes and its battle against birth defects.

When they entered, Mike and Don caused a stampede among the hundreds of reporters and photographers who had turned out to cover the event. But Mike did more than just show up for dinner. He also agreed to serve as a celebrity chef, and he even won an award for his cooking skills from a panel of food critics that included Bryan Miller of *The New York Times*, Craig Claiborne, and Gael Greene.

The next day there were pictures in the paper of Mike dressed in a tuxedo and flipping flapjacks. But images like that never linger very long in people's minds. The public, and often the press, preferred to think of Mike as half-man, half-beast. A fighting machine.

That was an image created partly by Mike himself but mostly by the writers who published scathing articles and books about the young fighter. In many cases, these reporters and authors made a good living off Mike before they turned on him to make a few more bucks with their pathetic and exaggerated accounts. One such writer is José Torres, the former boxer and New York State athletic commissioner. Torres befriended Mike and worked with him, and to Mike's face he couldn't have been nicer. It turned out, though, that Torres used his taped conversations with Mike in a book that was an embarrassment for all concerned.

I know Mike Tyson well. In the period since my last book, I've staged his fights against Tyrell Biggs, Larry Holmes, Michael Spinks, and Carl "The Truth" Williams, and I was at ringside when he lost his title to Buster Douglas in Japan. I've also sat with the champ for many hours in offices, on airplanes, and at ringside at other people's fights. The Mike Tyson I know is very different from the guy I've seen portrayed in the press.

He's a professional warrior, yes, but he's no semi-human being who was born to fight.

Of course, Mike usually goes out of his way not to show his vulnerable side. He grew up on the mean streets, where any sign of weakness could be fatal. He has also been trained since the age of thirteen—when Cus D'Amato got hold of him and first started teaching him how to box—never to let the other guy know you're hurting, and to turn your self-doubt into desire.

Mike actually has a great attitude about fear, which he learned from Cus, a very wise man in addition to being a legendary fight trainer. "Fear is like fire," the old man used to say. "If you don't know how to handle it, it can kill you. But if you use it correctly, it can warm your house." That happens to be as true in the business world as it is in boxing.

What a lot of people have never understood about

Mike is that he considers boxing to be a twenty-four-hour-a-day job. Like a comedian who can't stop telling jokes, he is always on and, at least in terms of the impression he wants to give, always ready to rumble. For most of his life there has always been another fight looming in Mike's future, and that means there are always opponents out there, thinking about Mike Tyson and listening to every word he says. Mike understands that, and without sitting down and actually mapping out a strategy, he developed a way to use the press to gain a psychological edge over these prospective rivals.

Sometimes he did this with humor. In the dressing room after some of his early fights, Mike would say things like "When I hit him, he screamed like a woman," or "I just wanted to push his nose bone back into his brain." Mike knew those were ridiculous things to say, but he was hoping that the reporters would print his outrageous remarks and that his next opponent would read them and become a beaten man right then and there. In some instances, it was a pure put-on of the press, though that often backfired. The sportswriters and TV reporters never realized that Mike, a bit bored with the same old questions, was actually doing a parody of a postfight interview. They would use his responses, but as examples of what a tough warrior he was.

I got a kick out of watching him, because cultivating a "killer" image is not unknown to dealmakers. A smart man or woman knows that if the other party thinks you are invincible, he may not even bother asking for certain things.

Good businessmen and seasoned boxers should both take such tough talk in stride—and yet for a while Mike got tremendous results with that gambit every time. For example, I don't think I've ever seen a guy as psyched out before a fight as Michael Spinks was as he prepared to fight Tyson. The minute and a half that Spinks spent in the ring with Iron Mike was a mere technicality. Despite being an intelligent guy—or maybe *because* he had so much good sense—Spinks got dismantled, mentally, even before he stepped into the ring.

For some reason, though, Buster Douglas was never scared of Mike, and it showed. Maybe it was because Douglas was preoccupied with thoughts of his mother, who had died about a month before he faced Tyson. Or perhaps Buster was thinking about his young child's mother, who had just been diagnosed as having a rare and possibly fatal kidney disease. Or maybe Buster is just a lot braver than anyone gives him credit for being. Whatever the reason, he fought, from the opening bell, as if he'd never heard the rumor that Tyson was the greatest of all time.

As much as I like Mike, and though I have a business interest in his future fights at my hotel-casinos, I have to say that Douglas fought a truly beautiful fight—the kind that brings to mind the term "sweet science."

He didn't brawl. He didn't lose his cool and start throwing those big but ineffective roundhouse punches. Rather, he continually set things up with his crisp left jab and followed through with his stinging right. Until then, all of Mike's opponents had been worried about getting hurt. Douglas was the first guy who realized that the best defense was a sensational nonstop offense.

Very few people, including Mike himself, could accept the fact that Tyson simply got beat. Around where I was sitting, people starting yelling, "It was fixed. He was drugged." Later, there was a brief controversy over whether Tyson had been victimized by a long count. But in the end, everyone realized that however many seconds had elapsed, the larger truth was that Mike Tyson just wasn't the better boxer that Sunday afternoon in Japan.

I *am* anxious about what happens next for Mike. No matter whom he fights in the years ahead, he faces his greatest challenge now. In a world that asks, "What have you done lately?" he can only respond, "I lost the big one." For a long while he was Superman, or at least everyone told him he was. Now, if he wants to feel good about himself, he'll have to find a way to define himself by something other than his ring record. That's okay, because he'd have to do that sooner or later anyway. I just hope Mike hasn't been too twisted out of shape by his earlier years of unblemished success.

Mike does have some unusual habits and attitudes, especially when it comes to money. He is totally uninterested in it. There were times when I'd talk to him about financial planning, tax shelters, and investments, and I'd see by the look in his eyes that I'd lost him completely. It wasn't that he couldn't follow what I was saying. He just doesn't have the slightest interest in the subject.

Soon after the Spinks fight I presented Mike with a check for $10 million. He said thank you, folded it, and put it in his jacket pocket without glancing at it —it was no big deal. A few days later one of my accountants called me and said that the check had never been cashed and that we had better find out what was going on.

It turned out that Mike had simply misplaced the $10 million. When someone reminded him about it, he shrugged and looked for the check, but it was a few weeks before it was found and deposited by one of his people.

Because of the way Mike treats money, a lot of people have predicted that he'll be taken advantage of and left penniless, like so many heavyweight champions before him. Until I got to know Mike better, I used to say that myself. Now I believe that won't happen. Because of his street smarts, Mike will always know who's trying to take advantage of him and who's on his side—and I pity the guy who tries to rip him off. Yes, he gave a Bentley to a meter maid and a Rolls-Royce to a couple of policemen without thinking twice, and when those stories got retold in the newspapers, he seemed to be out of control. But the truth is that those two cars constituted a tiny fraction of Mike's net worth; giving them away was about the same as an average working person's parting with a pair of roller skates.

In any case, those incidents date back to a time in Mike's life when he was extremely confused. I'm talking, of course, about his brief but troubled marriage to actress Robin Givens.

The particulars of that period have been hashed over so many times in the press that by now everyone is familiar with the public story. Suffice it to say that Mike, who is normally a picture of mental toughness, came completely apart at the seams during his marriage. One night, at a point when things were happening fast and furiously, Mike called me at home. I told him to try to get a grip on himself. "Listen, Mike," I said, "you've got to ask yourself how you really feel about this woman."

"Mr. Trump," he replied, sounding as confused as ever, "I just love that fucking bitch."

I don't believe, though, that there were heroes and villains in this story. Despite the way they were portrayed in the news media, his wife, Robin, and her mother, Ruth Roper, were not evil women; in fact, they indirectly made a lot of money for Mike by insisting, as a matter of principle, that he get a bigger cut in his management contract with Bill Cayton.

At the same time, though, there was something about Robin that drove Mike crazy. She is an extremely beautiful woman, and Mike was fascinated and in a way intoxicated by that. I was very close to them during those difficult months, and they both turned to me at different times to express their feelings. I don't think I'm violating a confidence if I say that Mike's problem was that he was much more in love with the outer Robin than with the inner one. But what matters most now to both him and Robin is that the marriage is over and the turmoil has subsided.

The one pitfall Mike must avoid in the future is the common mistake of thinking that success in one area means you're an all-around genius. Unless he undergoes a major personality change, Mike will never be a good businessman. For a while I had planned to be Mike's financial adviser, something I would do for Mike, purely out of friendship, and probably for no one else. I soon realized, however, that this could never really happen because of Mike's total lack of interest in money. There would be no use in my talking about personal finances if no one was listening. My message to Mike for a long time now has been simple: Stay out of investments, real estate deals, and tax shelters. Just put some of your money into Treasury bills and the rest into a solid bank, I've told him (though there are fewer and fewer of those around). Why should Mike try to earn more than 8 percent on his money when his income is $50 million to $100 million a year and he needs very little on which to live?

Any discussion of Mike's affairs eventually leads to the subject of Don King. Don, like Mike, is something of an enigma. The difference between the two is that Don delights in being one; he likes keeping people a bit off balance all the time because it usually works to his advantage.

Don is always onstage, with his wild hairdo and penchant for long, rambling speeches and big words. This act of his has led a lot of people to ask me what Don King is really like behind closed doors at the end of a long, hard negotiating session. To that I can only say, "Believe it or not, he's exactly the same." That bombastic persona comes naturally to him, and because he knows that he can wear people down and frustrate them with it, he's not about to change.

Don's dealings with Mike proceeded in the classic manner of fighter-promoter relationships. When I first heard about the future heavyweight champ, he was a young kid being managed by Bill Cayton and Jim Jacobs, partners in an advertising agency as well as a company that owned the world's largest collection of fight films. Don King was in the picture but playing a minor role as Mike's promoter. When Jacobs died, Don King immediately moved in and tried to convince

Mike that the fighter was making a mistake by staying with Cayton. I know Bill, and I believe he is a true gentleman who always had Mike's interests at heart. But I also realize that he is an older man whose background is very different from Mike's. He could never relate to Mike the way that Don can. When King moved in on the young fighter, it really wasn't much of a contest.

Though he comes off as clownish at times, Don is tough and very serious about his goals. It doesn't matter to him in the slightest that he's hated by many people or that he has a reputation among the general public as a con man *extraordinaire*. The fact is that he's not. He's a shrewd and hardened businessman. When a big fight is being discussed, he knows how to play me against my rivals in Las Vegas, and how to play all the Las Vegas interests against one another. He also has a fanaticism about beating the white establishment at its own game, and though that doesn't work in my interest financially, I happen to think it's admirable. As long as he plays fair and keeps his word—which he does with me—I can't complain that he plays the angles and drives a hard bargain.

Don can be just as tough and hard with his fighters as he is with the people who are negotiating for his events. Don is not a maker of champions. He takes fighters who have reached the top away from other managers and promoters. Even fighters as experienced and street-smart as Roberto Durán and Larry Holmes have been convinced by Don, through a combination of salesmanship and sheer tenacity, to forget their former connections and cast their lot with him. Often he does take them to new heights. But if a fighter tries to cross Don or to violate his contract, he's going to realize he's not dealing with a guy who's just a clown. Buster Douglas and his manager, Jimmy Johnson, found that out when they tried to get out of a binding deal they signed with King Enterprises. Don clearly has a right to promote a Tyson-Douglas rematch, and he's not going to walk away from what promises to be one of the great heavyweight clashes of the century.

How will Don King treat Mike Tyson in the long run? Bill Cayton had an interesting response to that question. "Mike is suffering from the Patty Hearst syndrome," he told a reporter. "He's fallen in love with his captor."

Only time will tell how the King-Tyson relationship works out, but right now I'm not worried about Mike. One reason is that Don has a tremendous affection for the still-very-young fighter; his desire to protect Mike at all costs is almost an obsession. I've never seen Don anywhere near as devoted to anyone else.

The other reason I believe Mike won't get hurt is because Mike is no fool. This is a man who learned at a very early age to take care of himself. Shortly after he had that famous early-morning altercation with a former opponent named Mitch "Blood" Green in a Harlem clothing store, I spoke to Mike on the phone and asked him if it had really been necessary to resort to physical violence. Mike sounded incredulous. "Mr. Trump," he said, "the guy was coming at me, trying to hurt me. I *had* to take him out." Mike may not give a damn about fluctuations in the gold market or pork-belly futures, but he knows when someone's trying to hurt him. As long as he doesn't do anything to hurt himself, he's going to be all right.

PART
III

TWELVE

ON TOUGHNESS

I have a reputation for being tough, and I'd like to think it's justified. You *must* be tough when a lot of influential people are saying that your day has come and gone, when your marriage is breaking up, and when business pressures are increasing. Toughness, in the long run, is a major secret of my survival. But I also realize that a lot of people who throw around the term have no idea what it really means.

When I try to define toughness, I often conjure up a mental image of the great football running backs of years past. These were not gentle men—yet no one ever accused them of being unfair. Sometimes you saw them just plowing ahead, sometimes sidestepping, sometimes spinning off blockers, and sometimes straight-arming opponents. Like all the great athletes (and all great business people), they knew the textbook plays, but they weren't afraid of going out and making up moves as they went along. They almost never used the same tactic twice—and yet one thing never changed. They were always moving forward, and with great determination, toward the goal at which they, as much as anyone else, were aiming.

Toughness, as I see it, is a quality made up of equal parts of strength, intelligence, and self-respect. I think I became intrigued with the quality as I grew up and watched what was happening to my older brother, Fred, a great and talented guy who had a career as an airline pilot but who died of alcoholism a few years ago. Fred, though I loved him dearly, was not traditionally tough. He was sweet and trusting, and as a result, people constantly took advantage of him. Watching what happened to Fred, I learned to study people closely and always to keep my guard up, in both my personal and my professional life. Fred was truly one of my great teachers.

Occasionally, yes, toughness *does* involve some old-fashioned ass-kicking. There are times, for example, when on the spur of the moment I'll dial the number of one of my hotels or the Trump Shuttle, just to see how long it takes my people to answer the phone. If I have to wait for more than five or six rings, I'll tell the employee who finally does answer who I am. Then I'll ask—without hiding my annoyance—what the problem is. I've found that usually that person will not have to be reminded about the standards I expect.

Yet despite what many people think, being tough has nothing to do with bullying people. A bully to me is someone who is trying to work out some psychological problem by intimidating others. The real estate business, especially in New York, is full of bullies— people who've gotten somewhere in the past by screaming, and so they keep on screaming at their adversaries, their employees, their spouses. Leona Helmsley is a bully who is driven mostly by a desire to intimidate others or to get away with something that other people can't. Being a good businesswoman is, to her, secondary to being a bitch on wheels.

Usually I'm friendly, polite, and upbeat in my dealings with employees and even with business adversaries. I don't recommend speaking sternly to people or throwing your weight around unless it serves some clear purpose. If, in the course of conducting one of my spot checks, I find the Trump Shuttle phone system less than perfect and express my displeasure or even my anger, I'm just taking care of business in an honest fashion. I'm not going behind anyone's back to complain or have someone fired. We've had a minute of unpleasantness, perhaps, but then the air is cleared and we can all get back to business.

I admire toughness in people such as Rupert Murdoch, Steve Ross, Ace Greenberg, Ron Perelman,

Marty Davis of Paramount, Jack Welch of G.E., and others. Those are men who expect to succeed and who understand the ins and outs of maintaining success, but they don't feel out of their element when things aren't going well; they are capable of taking a losing proposition and turning it around.

I especially admire toughness in the people I'm negotiating with. Take a certain killer dealmaker with the unlikely name of Sister Cecilia.

I met Sister Cecilia a few years ago. Our paths crossed because she was in charge of the New York Foundling Hospital, a venerable Manhattan institution that stood for nearly one hundred years on the corner of Sixty-ninth Street and Third Avenue. That site was interesting to me because the Upper East Side had become, in the last ten years or so, an extremely exciting and desirable area, especially for single and affluent people who could take full advantage of the Manhattan life-style. But I wouldn't have thought of approaching Sister Cecilia about her real estate if I hadn't also observed that having her hospital in such a fashionable neighborhood, sitting on such valuable real estate, made less sense every day. After all, this was an institution that was trying to provide health care to the city's poor.

The idea I planned to discuss with Sister Cecilia was, I thought, good for both of us. I wanted to give her a great price for her site and then help her implement a plan by which the New York Foundling Hospital would be reorganized in the form of many smaller health care facilities that would be situated in poorer areas—downtown, Harlem, Brooklyn, and the South Bronx—where they were desperately needed. The fact that there was a great piece of real estate for me in the deal didn't make me any less proud of the idea, which I felt would help people and help stabilize some troubled neighborhoods.

I called Sister Cecilia's office and asked for an appointment. She agreed, but without the slightest trace of enthusiasm. I should have known right then that I was dealing with a tough customer.

Walking into her office was an experience I'll never forget. As I smiled and introduced myself, she looked at me sternly. I half expected, as I extended my hand in greeting, that she would rap me across the knuckles with a ruler.

Instead, though, she just said, "What is it you want?" Her eyes were piercing, her gray hair was pulled back tightly. Everything about her said, "Cut the preliminaries, buddyboy, and get to the point."

There was no warm-up time with this lady. Suddenly, I was center stage with the lights on and I had to do my number. But that was okay with me. I had thought long and hard about what I was going to say, and I believed very strongly in my plan.

"Sister," I said, "I want to run an idea by you. This neighborhood has changed. Virtually all of your patients have to travel a considerable distance to get to the hospital, and they have nowhere to go for help in their own areas. On top of that, you need money to continue what you do.''

From there I went on to explain my plan in detail. I knew that just about every other developer in New York City was salivating over her site, and no doubt some had approached her already, dangling big sums before her. I thought I had the advantage of them for several reasons. I had an idea for what the hospital might do with the money I was offering; I had a plan to put up a beautiful building in place of the outdated hospital structure; and I had an excellent track record for getting things done.

I don't think I've ever pitched something more skill-fully. I gave a ten-minute presentation into which I packed all the salesmanship, charm, and dealmaking ability I could muster. Then I turned to her and asked, ''So, Sister, what do you think?''

And she just said, ''No.''

Not ''You'll have to come up with a better offer,'' or ''This is happening so fast, I'll have to think about it and get back to you.'' Just ''No.'' Then she turned back to her work, making it clear I was dismissed.

This, I knew, was one tough lady.

Fortunately for me, I happen to be a very persistent guy. In analyzing the situation, I realized that there was nothing wrong with my plan or the offer I'd made. The problem, I concluded, was that as far as she was concerned, I was just some guy walking in off the street and making big promises. What I needed was someone to put me in the right context, so my reputation could work for me—in other words, a proper introduction.

I let some time pass, because I didn't want to come off as a nuisance to the Foundling Hospital people and because I was busy with a lot of other things. But while I was waiting, the New York archdiocese announced that it was selling the site and that it had hired a consulting firm to help market the property. The first thing I did when I heard this news was to call a good friend of mine, Bill Fugazy.

Bill founded one of New York's most famous limousine companies, and he's a great guy to play golf with, but the reason I called him that day is that he has a sister who's a Catholic nun. Her name is Sister Irene, and because she runs the ITV, which is the Catholic TV network in New York, she's got connections with everyone in the Church.

"Bill," I said to my friend, "I'd like your sister to give Sister Cecilia a call on my behalf. I'm very interested in the Foundling Hospital property."

"So is every other real estate guy in New York," Bill said. "But the archdiocese has made a rule. They printed an elaborate brochure about the hospital property, and they're not taking any bids until the brochure goes out in the mail."

"Just give me your sister's number," I said to him. "I'll take it from there."

I was perfectly honest with Sister Irene. "I want to buy the hospital site," I said. "But the first time I talked to Sister Cecilia, she killed me. She practically threw me out. I haven't been treated like that since I got out of college."

"Now, now, my son, calm down," Sister Irene said. "Sister Cecilia is a saintly woman. She's just looking out for the hospital's best interest. I'll give her a call on your behalf and see what I can do."

A short time later she called back and said that Sister Cecilia would be happy to meet with me to discuss the hospital site. I couldn't believe the change in attitude. But I wasn't taking anything for granted, either. As added insurance, when I went to meet with her I called another friend, Bill Flynn, the head of Mutual Insurance Company of America. In addition to being a staunch Irish Catholic, Bill was also the chairman of the Foundling Hospital board.

Don't let anyone ever tell you that having the proper connections isn't important. The difference between my first and my second meetings with Sister Cecilia was like night and day. I made my presentation all over again, and I ended up making a deal with her and Bill Flynn quickly and effectively. Meanwhile, the week after my visit, that brochure went into the mail, and the other developers began ringing Sister Cecilia's phone off the hook. A lot of them, I understand, were pretty angry when they found out that Donald Trump had already signed a deal for the site.

* * *

The opposite of toughness—weakness—makes me mad and sometimes turns my stomach. I'm not referring here to the kind of weakness that comes from being poor, sick, or disadvantaged. I'm talking about those people who can take a strong stand but just don't. That's why I've started to speak out about what is happening to America, particularly on the business front.

These days, with communism in retreat almost everywhere, it's tempting to think that the game is over and America has won. I don't see it that way. Our problems don't get solved just because the Eastern bloc's system suddenly falls apart. That's victory by default. If we give ourselves credit for triumphing, and fail to address the challenges that are before us on the international business and economic scene, America's role as the leading nation in the free world will be in serious jeopardy in the next ten or fifteen years.

The United States has a great system of government and a beautiful philosophy to go with it. Our problem is that we've stood behind our ideals only sporadically in recent years. President Reagan's mass firing of the air traffic controllers in 1981 comes to mind as an example of standing firm for a principle, as does our invasion of Grenada in 1983 and, even more important, President Bush's military action that brought Manuel

Noriega from Panama to an American jail in December 1989. To me, however, our bombing of Muammar Qaddafi's headquarters in Libya stands out as a classic case of how effective a tough stance for a valid purpose can be in the area of international politics. Think about it: Qaddafi, for years one of the great villains of the modern world, has hardly been heard from since those shells started exploding.

But the record proves you don't always have to resort to missiles and rifles to get your point across. In fact, as the twentieth century comes to a close, the greatest challenges and threats we face are economic ones—and they are coming from two of our supposed allies, Japan and Germany.

I do a great deal of business with both those countries. The Japanese are regular customers for my real estate and frequent visitors to my casinos. The Japanese and the Germans hold some of my loans. I know they will understand that by speaking out, what I'm really advocating is that in our competitive zeal we be more like them, people and nations for whom I have a lot of respect.

The Japanese and the Germans are not the kinds of adversaries whom you face with weapons. Yet a wartime mentality may be just what we need to adopt when dealing with them. We have to think in terms of victory. The objective is not to vanquish those countries, as we did in World War II. It is to bolster ourselves.

Before we can prevail, we need to believe that these countries are not destined always to get their way. A big part of our problem is that we *expect* the Japanese to get the better of us. This gives them a tremendous psychological advantage. We think they are always destined to be the winner. But that's not the way it has to be.

Not long ago I read a story in the paper saying that the Japanese were using unusually large nets in their commercial fishing operations. These nets, in the opinion of the other countries fishing in the same international waters, not only gave the Japanese an unfair advantage but also had a harmful effect on the environment because they led to the overharvesting of certain fish. Faced with that situation, the other countries might just have said, "Well, the Japanese, they're on top right now, they're strong, they do what they want." But instead, those countries got together, filed a strong protest with the proper authorities, and complained loudly to the press. In no time at all, the Japanese backed down and said they'd use the regulation nets again and observe the same rules and customs as everyone else did.

The point is that sometimes what you have to do is ask, and—if you display enough determination—what you want will eventually be given to you. You also have to be persistent. If asking once doesn't work, my suggestion is to ask again—perhaps a little more emphatically—and again and again and again.

In my first book I told the story of how I got a forty-year tax abatement from New York City when converting the old Commodore Hotel on Forty-second Street into the Grand Hyatt. "How did you ever get *forty years*?" people asked me.

"Because," I answered with a shrug, "I didn't ask for fifty."

Too many politicians today don't understand that unless they stand up and say clearly what they want in a particular situation, they can't expect to get it. Or, more likely, they do understand that, but by nature they are weak or worried about offending some special interest and they shrink from any kind of confrontation. As a result, they deal exclusively in compromises and limp concessions. That's why in the eyes of the rest of the world—even some of our supposed allies—when it comes to business, we've become a nation whose big dumb heart can constantly be taken advantage of.

The Japanese don't miss a trick when dealing with us. They have import quotas and tariffs to protect their own interests, and they even have ways of sealing up the cracks left by their official policies to make sure almost no American goods get into their country.

I know a man in the automobile business who told me that he had exported some cars to Japan, not with much hope of actually selling them there, but more as an experiment, just to see what would happen. When his shipload of American cars arrived at the dock, he found that the Japanese would need to thoroughly inspect his vehicles, ostensibly for their potential impact on the environment. How thorough are the Japanese in this regard? Well, they don't just check one car and figure that all of the others made on the same assembly line must be virtually identical. Instead, they look at each car, taking the engine apart, putting it back together, and running various tests. My acquaintance in the auto business estimated that at the rate they proposed to go, the Japanese inspectors would get through perhaps one car a day. That meant that his ship would be sitting in the harbor for six or seven months before they had tested all of his cars and authorized them to be brought into the country. Under those circumstances, he had no choice but to order the ship to return to America, still fully loaded.

Now, isn't it amazing that the most efficient country in the world can't figure out a way to unload a ship in less than half a year? But of course that's only part of the story. While the Japanese keep us from selling American-made cars in their country, Americans are buying tens of thousands of Toyotas, Nissans, and Hondas. One day not long ago I read two interesting reports in the same newspaper. One said that U.S. automakers were suffering through extremely tough times. The other noted that the Toyota Motor Corporation had nearly $12 billion in cash in its corporate war chest—and that one of its biggest problems at the moment was finding something to do with all that money.

Think about it: The ten largest banks in the world are all Japanese, and the largest bank in America, Citibank, ranks about twenty-seventh on the list. The trade imbalance with Japan is costing us, by my estimate, about $100 billion a year. Some may dispute that number, which is somewhat higher than the official figure, but no one denies that the situation is totally out of control. Yet what do we do in response? Well, we meet with Japan's representative and come away with promises of increased trade opportunities but very few specifics and no timetable. Then, as if that weren't bad enough, when the prime minister gets back to Japan, the leading politicians tell him that he promised President Bush things he had no right to promise and that, essentially, the deal, which really wasn't much of a deal, is off. Meanwhile, the United States is losing millions of dollars a day and no one is doing anything about it.

What really shocks me, though, is when I hear a man like Roger Smith, the head of General Motors, knocking his own product and praising the Japanese. Oh, yes, the Japanese make a truly great car, Smith said on a nationally televised show I happened to be watching not long ago. Then he added that GM wasn't up to that standard yet, but he fully intended it to be . . . someday.

I know Roger Smith could never have risen to the top of such a huge corporation if he were really as weak as he sounded on that show. But the time has come to stop being diplomatic and always playing Mr. Nice Guy toward our trade rivals. Smith must realize that when an adversary can see fear in your eyes or hear it in your voice, you're as good as gone. A person may be able to survive in politics or a State Department job with no discernible talent, but in business— whether you're a man or a woman—you must have a quality for which there is, unfortunately, no better term than "balls."

It's one thing to admire Japan for how far it has come in the decades since it was defeated in World War II. But many Americans are absolutely in awe of the Japanese. They feel that these people are somehow destined to take over the world economically and that there is no way they can be stopped. This attitude reminds me of how people used to talk about the Russians. They were wrong then, and I think they're wrong about the Japanese now.

Not long ago I got a call from an old friend whose voice, from the first hello, had that I-need-a-big-favor tone. Normally, I wouldn't have minded helping this particular caller with almost anything. I have a real soft spot for this guy. He's a stockbroker who always works hard and means well, even though many people, including his own wife, see him as one of life's perennial losers. But this time the favor he wanted was pretty big.

"Donald," he said, "you've got to help me. I'd like you to have a meeting with a man who's probably the second or third wealthiest man in Japan."

"Why?" I asked.

"Because he said he wanted to see you, and I told him I might be able to arrange it."

"Oh, you did?" I said. "What does he want?"

"Just to ask you a few questions."

"Listen, I'm very busy," I said.

But he persisted. "Donald, you don't understand. This is very important to me for business reasons."

"I can't."

"But please . . ."

And as the conversation went on, he got more and more emphatic, until I finally agreed to meet the man from Japan in my office later that week. (Incidentally, there's a lesson here: In business, as in life, there is more than one way to get what you want. As soon as I'd hung up the phone it struck me that my friend's "loser" image may be something he cultivates and uses as a negotiating tool. If so, I guess it worked this time. But appearing to be weak is not a tactic that I'd recommend to anyone who is interested in success over the long haul.)

I put all thoughts of the wealthy Japanese businessman out of my mind until a few days later, when, deeply absorbed in some work at my desk, I suddenly heard a commotion in my outer office. It sounded as if the New York Mets were paying me a surprise visit.

The first thing I saw when I looked up was a guy slowly backing into my office with a video camera on his shoulder. The camera was pointed at the door. This photographer was followed by a man who was holding a still camera and clicking away madly. The second guy seemed to be taking pictures of everything in sight—including the first guy.

What the hell is going on here? I wondered. It was incredible—no one had knocked or waited to be announced; they'd just barged in. But I couldn't get too mad at those two photographers. They were just doing their job, which was, apparently, to record the entrance into my office of One of the Wealthiest Men in Japan.

It was a good thing they'd brought a lot of film. The main guy didn't walk in right away. He was preceded by probably eleven or twelve underlings, each one looking like a high-powered businessman in his own right. But no—when their very intense-looking boss finally did enter, all of the men in the entourage acted like butlers and bodyguards, taking the wealthy man's coat, sliding a chair under him, and so forth. As I sat there watching this spectacle, I thought that the people who believe *I* get pampered should see this.

There were more surprises to come. My wealthy

Japanese visitor didn't even say good morning to me; he just started speaking.

"I want real estate," he stated.

"What?" I asked.

"I want real estate for investment purpose."

Hearing this, I shot a glance at my friend the broker, who had slipped into my office with this man's entourage. He looked back uneasily, as if to say, This is going to be a rough meeting, isn't it, Donald?

I wanted to say, No, not really. But it sure as hell is going to be a short one.

I then turned to my visitor, smiled, and said, "The relationship between your country and mine has changed greatly in our lifetimes, hasn't it?"

His answer came quickly and matter-of-factly. "Oh, yes, Japan used to be down here," the man said, gesturing toward the floor, "and America was up here. Now, Japan is up here and America is way down there. We no longer admire your country the way we used to. But I came to talk about real estate for investment purpose."

At that point I stood up and told my very surprised visitor that I felt it was time for him and his people to leave.

I hadn't thrown anyone out of my office in quite a while. But it felt good. I didn't have any qualms about showing them all to the door because the wealthy Japanese gentleman was, to say the least, extremely rude.

I only wish that I could say he was wrong, too.

* * *

Americans simply don't get the respect and deference we deserve as a great power, the undisputed leader in both military and economic strength. I thought it was brilliant when Saudi Arabia and Kuwait—countries in which many people live in mansions—stood by and allowed us to police the Persian Gulf for them (free of charge). In South Korea there are often incidents in which our troops are abused and assaulted on the streets—even as Americans are buying huge quantities of Korean-made VCRs, computers, and TVs.

The Germans have treated us even worse, if that's possible. For two generations American troops have provided security for West Germany against the Soviets, but if an American tried to sell a pencil on the street in Germany, the authorities would practically throw him in jail. Meanwhile, those same Germans are sending their Mercedeses over here as fast as they can make them. And the situation is getting more serious. By 1992, the Europeans will have formed an economic union that will make doing business in that part of the world even more difficult for us than it is now. At the same time, East and West Germany are embarked on reunification, which looms as very bad news for the rest of the world. Just look at the reaction of Germany's neighbors. From the moment the Berlin Wall crumbled, Britain and France have been deeply concerned about the ramifications of a single German nation. The United States should be worried as well, given Germany's twentieth-century history of trouble, not to mention its lack of fairness toward America in recent years. But, predictably, we—still the most important and potentially most influential nation in the world (but fading fast)—are once again sitting on the sidelines and doing nothing except waiting to be taken advantage of.

The ironic thing is, there is no shortage of people out there who understand the need for business toughness. In the era since the Vietnam war we have witnessed the rise of a generation of driven, intense, and sometimes ruthless individuals who came out of college and totally rewrote the rules of doing business in this country. Yet in our dealings with the rest of the world we've too often become a bunch of suckers.

That's why I'm now making a modest proposal.

I think America should call on its corporate leaders, independent dealmakers, and other nonpolitical public figures who emerged during the past two decades to help us forge a new relationship with the rest of the world. I'm suggesting that these people form a kind of all-star panel that would oversee America's negotiations with Japan, Europe, and other areas needing special attention. The blue-ribbon volunteers would be vested with as much authority as our Constitution would permit.

Listed below are some of the people I'd choose for this job. I have watched them work, and in some cases

I've negotiated with them one-on-one. I can assure you that, if given a free rein, they could reverse America's eroding economic status and enhance our country's stature as a role model for the rest of the world in a matter of months.

Jack Welch, of General Electric
Henry Kravis of Kohlberg Kravis Roberts, the country's leading practitioner of leveraged buyouts
Steve Ross of Time Warner
Martin Davis, chairman of Paramount Communications
Bob or Sid Bass, investors *extraordinaires*
Michael Eisner, CEO of Disney
Ron Perelman, another LBO wizard, who owns Revlon
Ted Turner, the broadcaster
Carl Icahn, the boss of TWA

If I were selected to serve on this council, I know the first thing I'd propose: the imposition of a 20 percent tax on imports from Japan, Germany, and other countries that don't play by the rules. That money—which would amount to billions of dollars—could reduce the federal deficit and pay for education, housing, and medical care in poor areas throughout America. So what if the Japanese slapped a tax on us in response? The fact is, the effect would be negligible because we buy a whole lot more from the Japanese than we sell them.

Even as I write this, I can hear the howls of protest from the foreign businessmen who'd be affected—and can see them pounding on the doors of senators and congressmen, demanding to be heard. But I wouldn't feel pressured by those tactics, as the politicians involved no doubt would. Rather, I would take that strong reaction as an indication that I'd done the right thing. And then I'd move on to the next case.

America has been weak not just in dealing with other nations but in dealing with our internal troubles, such as drug abuse and rampant crime. I find this especially frustrating because from the mail I receive and the people I talk to—security guards, executives, construction workers—I get a sense that virtually everyone in America is sick of the lack of progress in solving those problems. They want action. And yet the prevailing wisdom among politicians seems to be that taking too tough a stand can be hazardous to a person's political career.

That really came home to me about a year ago, when I got involved in the debate over capital punishment. What happened, as some people will recall, was that a young woman who worked as an executive on Wall Street was brutally beaten and raped by a gang of young men while she was jogging in Central Park.

That terrible incident had almost everybody in the city talking about how crime was out of control and how law enforcement officials were handcuffed by a system that ensured only the criminal's rights and kept the police in constant fear of facing charges of brutality. To my astonishment, though, some newspaper columnists and others actually leapt to the defense of the gang members. To these misguided people, the muggers and rapists were "the real victims" because of such "underlying causes" as poverty, a lack of educational opportunities, and so forth.

Without minimizing the plight of many people in our inner cities, that's ridiculous. The people who assaulted that jogger, and then laughed about it after the police had picked them up, were, in my opinion, one step removed from animals. I thought that if the woman had died, they would have deserved to be executed for what they'd done—and I took a full-page ad in *The New York Times* to say so.

As soon as the ad appeared, I got calls from seven or eight top politicians, congratulating me for taking a stand and saying they agreed with my position. These were very prominent people—household names— with much power and influence to get things changed.

"So, why don't you take a similar position publicly?" I asked each one of them. "You hold a high public office; you have a vote in your legislative body. I'm sure you could do some good."

But each one responded in virtually the same way:

"Oh, gee, I'd like to, Donald, but it's such a controversial issue. When you're in politics, it's touchy. You can't really come down hard on things like this anymore."

Ed Koch, who was then still mayor of New York, had the typical politician's reaction to my ad. While expressing the obligatory outrage, he said that he had "controlled anger" toward the criminals who'd beaten the woman jogger within an inch of her life, and that he didn't believe in hate.

I *do* believe in hate when it's appropriate, and I think this is one of those occasions. No one cares about Ed Koch's opinions anymore. I think it's much more telling that since that ad appeared I've received well over fifteen thousand letters of support for my position on capital punishment.

Whenever I've taken a stand like that in public, people ask me if I have any plans to run for elective office. The answer is no. I'm not a politician. I wouldn't want to get involved in the compromises, the glad-handing, and all the other demeaning things you have to do to get votes. Most of the best people we've had in government lately have, I've noticed, been appointed to their posts.

But do I think I could get elected? At one time I would have said yes, probably. But now, since my marital problems and business pressures have been dragged through the newspapers, I'm less sure. In any case, I'd have to face one big obstacle if I ever did make a serious run for public office: Americans have become so accustomed to professional politicians that when they are faced with a strong personality—a man or woman of action—they are afraid, or at least very wary.

The fact is that there is a certain logic in the professional politicians' reluctance to take a strong stand. Toughness is scary. A brilliant man like General Douglas MacArthur would never be allowed to rise to power in the America of today. (I can imagine MacArthur hearing about "a thousand points of light" and assuming Bush was talking about laser weapons.)

When we fear leaders of great passion, though, what we often forget is that the other side fears them too. I remember reading that Hitler, as he rose to power during his early years, continually talked to the people around him about Winston Churchill. "Keep an eye on that man," he kept saying. "He's going to be one of our biggest problems." The English politicians criticized Churchill for calling Hitler a mad dog; it wasn't diplomatic—in fact, they said, it was downright inflammatory. Yet Hitler, in his way, respected Churchill, whom he recognized as not just another government official but rather an advocate for the English people—a man who would never stop pushing and pressuring until he got what he wanted. And Hitler was right about that, of course. When Hitler's people told him that Churchill was politically dead, no longer a problem, Hitler stated that Churchill would emerge—"People like that never die."

One of our biggest problems today is that we have too few advocates. What we have instead are too many weaklings and compromisers.

I respect smart, tough people the way others admire great athletes or entertainers—even when these people are unpopular or down on their luck. That's why, when John Connally, the former governor of Texas, phoned my office about a year ago, I took the call immediately. I'd met John Connally and shaken his hand once or twice, but I didn't really know him, so I was a little surprised when in the course of a very friendly conversation, he made a request. His wife, Nell, was going to be honored at a dinner, he said. It was going to be a very big night in Houston, and he wanted to know if I'd serve as honorary chairman of the event.

As I've already said, I'm not crazy about travel or about serving as chairman of big charity affairs. I often send a contribution on the condition that I don't have to show up for the event, even if it's someplace in Manhattan. But Connally was a man who had fascinated me ever since he was wounded at the time of President Kennedy's assassination in 1963. Later, when he was indicted in the so-called Milk Scandal of the early 1970s, I'd noticed that he remained calm, stated serenely that he was innocent, and was eventually cleared of all charges. More recently, John had experienced some severe financial hardships. He'd lost much of his money when the oil business went bad, and he had been forced to declare bankruptcy. I'll never forget watching a television news show and seeing John and Nell sitting, with pride and dignity, in the front row of an auction hall while all the belongings from their house were sold to the highest bidders.

I can't speak for Connally's skill or luck as a businessman, but talk about toughness! Here was a man who many people thought would be president—and a woman who could have been first lady—suffering a terrible embarrassment but continuing to hold their heads high. I knew, just watching the strength of character they displayed on that occasion, that they would both make it back. And the dinner John was inviting me to proved they already had. I accepted, and I'm very glad I did. The event was a huge success and a celebration of John Connally's endurance—a quality that is a particularly attractive form of toughness.

So, in the end, what is toughness, as I see it, midway through my life?

Toughness is pride, drive, commitment, and the courage to follow through on things you believe in, even when they are under attack. It is solving problems instead of letting them fester. It is being who you really are, even when society wants you to be somebody else. Toughness is walking away from things you want because, for one reason or another, acquiring them doesn't make sense.

Toughness is knowing how to be a gracious winner—and rebounding quickly when you lose.

For a nation, toughness means avoiding complacency, meeting and solving problems head-on, and being willing to use power for goals you know are honorable.

In business, toughness means playing by the rules but also putting those rules to work for you. It is looking at an adversary across the desk and saying, simply, No.

Sometimes, if you hang in there long enough and, as the boxing trainers always say, "keep punching till the bell," people take notice and give you a boost. An editorial in the June 8, 1990, edition of *The New York Times* said this:

[Trump] has given non-admirers plenty of reasons for the malicious glee with which they hear of his problems. Good at his business, at every opportunity he tells the world how good. He feels compelled to paint the name TRUMP on every acquisition. He flaunts his possessions—the biggest yacht, the biggest house, the grandest helicopter—and not long ago pronounced his intention of building the tallest building in the world. His main motive was not greed but triumph.

Arrogance? For sure, and yet in a world lacking individual heroes, even some of Donald's critics must confess to a sneaking respect for his insistence on being himself, however outrageous, and catch themselves hoping he'll find the strength and luck to escape.

As I've said repeatedly in my first book and in this one, I believe in working hard. I believe in being smart and not cute. I don't respect cheaters. My admiration is reserved for those who have achieved greatness and then topped themselves.

I'm never satisfied—which is my way of saying that there is a great deal I still want to do and believe I should do.

Some people are always saying that I can't go on like this forever, and that I'm at the beginning of the end. I'd rather see myself as being at the end of the beginning.

INDEX